# LINCOLNSHIRE

# LINCOLNSHIRE

# SUSANNA O'NEILL

First published 2012, reprinted 2015
This edition published 2024

The History Press
97 St George's Place, Cheltenham,
Gloucestershire, GL50 3QB
www.thehistorypress.co.uk

© Susanna O'Neill, 2012, 2015, 2024

The right of Susanna O'Neill to be identified as the Author
of this work has been asserted in accordance with the
Copyrights, Designs and Patents Act 1988.

All rights reserved. No part of this book may be reprinted
or reproduced or utilised in any form or by any electronic,
mechanical or other means, now known or hereafter invented,
including photocopying and recording, or in any information
storage or retrieval system, without the permission in writing
from the Publishers.

British Library Cataloguing in Publication Data.
A catalogue record for this book is available from the British Library.

ISBN 978 1 80399 776 6

Typesetting and origination by The History Press.
Printed and bound in Great Britain by TJ Books Limited, Padstow, Cornwall.

Trees for LYfe

# CONTENTS

| | | |
|---|---|---|
| | Acknowledgements | 7 |
| | Introduction | 9 |
| 1 | The Devil and his Serpent | 20 |
| 2 | The Wet and Wilds | 41 |
| 3 | Black Dogs and Strange Encounters | 63 |
| 4 | Giants and Heroes | 76 |
| 5 | Things that go Bump in the Lincolnshire Night | 90 |
| 6 | Witchcraft and Cunning | 115 |
| 7 | Yellowbelly Sayings and Superstitions | 131 |
| 8 | A Lincolnshire Year | 152 |
| | Bibliography | 182 |
| | Notes | 185 |
| | Index | 190 |

# ACKNOWLEDGEMENTS

I extend my thanks to everyone who has helped and supported me during the writing of this book. I have met and talked to many interesting people along my journey and wish to name a few here.

Mrs Rose Cole, Caister, was especially welcoming and I would like to thank her for her kind hospitality and useful information.

I would like to thank the Boston Grammar School for their tour of the library and Beast Yard, especially Rowan Druce who was kind enough to show me around and supply me with interesting information, and also Paul Marsh, the head teacher, for allowing me to take photographs and use them in this publication.

I wish to thank Mr Arthur Franks for his help and wonderful collection of photographs and videos of the Haxey Hood game, which he kindly let me use in this book.

I am very grateful to the staff at Lincoln's Museum of Lincolnshire Life, who gave me their time, and to Lincolnshire County Council who allowed me to photograph and publish the pictures of the witch artefacts they house at the museum.

Roger John Crisp deserves my thanks and a mention for the marvellous tour he conducted for me around the grounds of RAF Scampton. It was very informative and a lot of fun! Thank you also for allowing me to publish the photographs I took there.

The staff at Grimsby Central Library were very helpful and friendly, as were the staff at Lincoln Cathedral, especially Anne James, who helped me with dates and festivals. Kath Brown kindly sent me information concerning the Lincolnshire Stuff Ball, for which I was most grateful.

Thank you to Mrs Rogers from the Captain's Table at Dogdyke for your stories and the gentleman from Beesby Cottages for your time and information.

Thank you also to the owner of the Abbey House at Swineshead for your directions and help, the gentleman at Horsington, the lady at Tealby who showed me where to find the Devil's Chair, and the gentleman at Lower Burnham for his information about the well.

I would like to thank The History Press for allowing me to write for them and especially Beth Amphlett and Matilda Richards, who have patiently led me through the process.

Thank you to my brother James for his support and patience at being dragged round various historical sites. Also thank you to my friend Yann, for his continued encouragement, help and company along the way.

Most of all, thank you to Judy and Arthur O'Neill, without whom this book would never have been completed. Thank you for all your time, your proofreading, your ideas and input and, of course, your company through many trips around Lincolnshire. You are invaluable!

# INTRODUCTION

When I was bound apprentice in famous Lincolnshire
Full well I served my master, for more than seven year,
Till I took up to poaching as you shall quickly hear,
Oh, 'tis my delight on a shiny night
In the season of the year.

As me and my companions were setting of a snare,
'Twas then we spied the gamekeeper, for him we did not care,
For we can wrestle and fight, my boys, and jump o'er anywhere.
Oh, 'tis my delight on a shiny night
In the season of the year.

As me and my companions were setting four or five,
And taking on 'em up again, we caught a hare alive,
We took the hare alive, my boys, although the wood did steer.
Oh, 'tis my delight on a shiny night
In the season of the year.

I threw him on my shoulder and then we all trudged home,
We took him to a neighbour's house and sold him for a crown,
We sold him for a crown, my boys, but I need not tell you where!
Oh, 'tis my delight on a shiny night
In the season of the year.

Success to every gentleman that lives in Lincolnshire,
Success to every poacher that wants to sell a hare.
Bad luck to every gamekeeper that will not sell his deer.
Oh, 'tis my delight on a shiny night
In the season of the year.[1]

You will not meet a Lincolnshire native who has never heard of this old folk song, 'The Lincolnshire Poacher'. Dating from the 1700s or earlier, it has become akin to the National Anthem for Lincolnshire and is still sung and quoted often today. Having a wealth of countryside and open land, coupled with the poor wages labourers received, Lincolnshire was ripe for poaching, even when it was a crime punishable by death! Not quite the happy-go-lucky past time the song suggests but certainly a poignant reminder of days gone by.

Lincolnshire is a fascinating county, rich with history, folklore, character and peculiarities, aptly summed up by John Betjeman:

> Lincolnshire is…singularly beautiful and…a separate country. I would like to see it with its own flag and needing passports to get in.[2]

One of the largest counties in England, Lincolnshire measures nearly 6,000 square kilometres. It is the county with the highest number of bordering counties, which include Leicestershire, Rutland, Cambridgeshire, Norfolk, South Yorkshire and Nottinghamshire. On the east, the North Sea runs its entire length and to the north it is bounded by the Humber Estuary.

Before 1974 it was divided into three regions: Holland, Lindsey and Kesteven, but after this date these three areas unified. The northern part, however, was given the title Humberside, but this was reversed in 1996 and the area became known as North Lincolnshire and North East Lincolnshire.

> Lincolnshire has a reputation for remoteness and mysteriousness, for being somehow semi-detached from the rest of England and not quite in the swing of modern life, a place where old ways are preserved and old secrets kept.[3]

This book will give the reader a glimpse of these secrets, of the traditions of old and those that remain, of the tales of indigenous giants, battles with dragons and brushes with the Devil himself. We shall walk with witches, bogles, ghosts and the infamous Black Dog, and laugh along at the Yellowbelly humour and curiosities, for there is a veritable feast to gorge upon!

> An enquiry after a person's health is usually one of the opening gambits in a conversation: but have you noticed that Lincolnshire folk will rarely admit to being well? Usually their reply will be 'I'm really no-matters' (in indifferent health). On a good day they may answer 'I'm fair to middlin'' or 'I'm meggerin' oop now,' by which they mean they're getting better. 'I've a bad keal an' I keb soa much at night and feel reeal al-ovverish' (a cough, short of breath and shivery); 'I've hed a bad bout of mulleygrubs and can't git shutten on it' (stomach ache).[4]

Typical Lincolnshire countryside.

The Lincolnshire dialect is a wonderfully colourful tongue and, as with any others, once immersed into it, it is as easy to understand as your own.

Katherine Briggs relates as a moral the story of a young cock that crowed too loudly before his time and ended up being fed to the pigs. The fascinating thing about the story is that it is all told in dialect and is fantastic to read.

> Yaller-legg's cock'ril liv'd i' runt yard wi' owd white cock 'at was his feyther, an' red cock liv'd o' steäm-hoose side o' yard. An' won daay, when owd cock's sittin' crawin' upon crew-yard gaate, cock'ril gets up an' begins to craw an' all.
>
> 'Cock-a-doodle-doo.' Says owd cock. 'Kick-a-ee-a-ee,' says cock'ril: he couldn't craw plain yit, he was ower yung.[5]

The study of folklore does not usually necessitate the study of dialect, but it can add another dimension to the meanings behind the stories for a deeper understanding. There are many books which list the numerous words, phrases and meanings of the varied Lincolnshire dialect, far too many to list here but as a taster and for interest I include a handful.

*Aist*: are you?
*Albins*: perhaps or unable
*At-nowt*: on no account
*Batterfang*: a heavy blow
*Blash*: nonsense
*Bo'd*: a bird
*Bo'n*: burn
*Chelp*: cheek, cheekiness
*Dacker-down*: slow-down, if someone was going too fast
*Darkilings*: twilight
*Dossent*: was to not dare to do something
*Eadily*: insufficiency
*Fogo*: a nasty smell
*Frangy*: lively
*Fun*: found
*Gaain*: near
*Harr*: a sea mist
*Kelter*: rubbish
*Ivey-skivy*: to create uproar
*Jorum*: a large amount
*Larum*: a worthless story
*Mawps*: a daft person
*Nosker*: large
*Owd-hunks*: a mean person
*Pag*: to carry another on your back
*Quick-sticks*: immediately
*Raatherly*: seldom
*Scrudge*: to squeeze
*Slap*: to spill something
*Tiddy*: small
*Upskittle*: to knock something over
*Vaals*: presents offered to servants
*Wong*: to low land
*Wottle-days*: working days
*Yetten*: eaten

    Here lies Jimmy Lang
    Kilt by Death's stang,
    They brake his boäns
    Wi sticks an' stoänes
    His carcas they did mang
    We many a batterfang.[6]

This wonderfully onomatopoeic tongue makes the language of the place come alive and fortunately for us, there are plenty of written samples. For instance, the *Lincolnshire Life* magazine gives examples of farmer's dialect which illustrates some of these local words:

> Lawks a massey me! Farming has changed since I was a bairn! Few folk these days 'addle their keep' as 'higglers' (men who keep horses and work them for hire), waggoners or garthmen (who look after and feed animals). 'Addlings', not 'earnings', were wages; 'earnings' or 'hearings' was rennet used for cheese making![7]

The great poet Alfred Lord Tennyson was born in Lincolnshire, at Somersby, where his father was a rector in 1809. Of the many poems he wrote, here is an extract from one, 'Northern Farmer', in the Lincolnshire dialect:

> Dosn't thou 'ear my 'erse's legs, as they canters awaäy?
> Proputty, proputty, proputty – that's what I 'ears 'em saäy.
> Proputty, proputty, proputty – Sam, thou's an ass for thy paaïns:
> Theer's moor sense i' one o'is legs nor in all thy braaïns.
>
> Woä – theer's a craw to pluck wi' tha, Sam: yon's parson's 'ouse –
> Dosn't thou knaw that a man mun be eäther a man or a mouse?
> Time to think on it then; for thou'll be twenty to weeäk.
> Proputty, proputty – woä then woä – let ma 'ear mysén speäk.'[8]

Statue of Alfred Lord Tennyson, housed in Lincoln Cathedral gardens.

Statue commemorating John Wesley, situated towards the top of Albion Hill, Epworth.

The content of money making, marriage, love and property is all the better for being read in dialect!

Tennyson is not the only notable to claim a Lincolnshire heritage. John Whitgift, the Archbishop of Canterbury from 1583 to 1604, was born in Grimsby and William Byrd, the composer, was born in Lincoln in 1543. Everyone has heard that Margaret Thatcher's humble origins stem from an upbringing in Grantham, and the poet Elizabeth Jennings (1926-2001) was born in Boston. King Henry IV was born at Bolingbroke Castle and was often known by the name Henry Bolingbroke.

Other famous names include Hereward the Wake, William Cecil, Sir Isaac Newton, Sir John Franklin, Sir Joseph Banks, Chad Varah, John Wesley, William Stukeley, Jennifer Saunders, Neil McCarthy – just to name a few.

The *Lincolnshire Poacher* magazine[9] quotes a source who talks of a postcard written by the young Winston Churchill in August 1887. He was staying on holiday with his nanny in a boarding house in Skegness. The postcard was addressed to his mother and the lad was asking her for half a crown, but apparently on the reverse the nanny had written a note to the effect that he should not be sent any money as he had already wasted a good deal! This was not the last time Churchill visited Lincolnshire; he was invited many times to speak at different places around the county in the early 1900s, and sources say he had quite an affection for the place.

Lincolnshire even has two claims on King Arthur, according to Marc Alexander. One states that it was at Lincoln that King Arthur came 'secretly upon Tholdric and fell silently upon the Saxons'.[10] The second tells that King Arthur fought a battle in the district of Lindsey, then known as Linnius.

*The Lincolnshire Magazine* from the 1930s propounds this idea, mentioning a great soldier in Digby, although whether it is actually King Arthur or another is debatable:

At Chestnut Tree Corner, under the little triangle of green grass where the footpath goes off to the station, a great soldier lies buried with all his men. One day a man will come along who can see a silver tree growing there, and he will see this tree as he stands on Canwick Hill, a point twelve miles distant...when he gets to Chestnut Tree Corner he will find steps going down into the ground, which he will descend and there he will find this great soldier and his men asleep. He will awaken them and they will rise all up again and fight for the King at a time when they are sorely needed.[11]

This story is prevalent all across Britain, most counties claiming the sleeping warriors, such as Craig y Dinas, Glamorgan or Alderly Edge, Cheshire or under Richmond Castle in Yorkshire, but to name a few, and so it is nice to see it included in Lincolnshire's folklore.

Having been invaded and inhabited by various races throughout the centuries, several of Germanic stock, many of the placenames of Lincolnshire have traceable routes. Professor Stenton[12] studied particularly those of Danish origin. He states that the characteristic type of Danish name in Lincolnshire ends in 'by', an ancient word meaning 'settlement' or 'village' which, he explains, is why we have the term 'bye-law', originally referring to the local regulation of a village community. He then goes on to say that uncomplimentary nicknames are characteristic in Lincolnshire, for example: Scamblesby, 'the village of the shameless one'; Scawby, 'the village of the bald man'; Brocklesby, 'the village of the man without trousers'; Sloothby, 'the village of the good-for-nothing rascal'. Not all are uncomplimentary however, such as Somerby, 'the village of a man who has taken part in a summer army'.

Those places ending in 'thorpe', such as Skellingthorpe, referred to a settlement smaller than the nearby village; 'ing' denoted low wet grass or pastures; 'with' meant a wood; 'langworth' was long ford; 'worth' referred to a small enclosure. Some examples of Anglo-Saxon endings to place names include 'stead', meaning place; 'staple', denoting a market; and 'ley' a meadow.

Lincoln Cathedral.

Many places were named after certain people or families such as Hagworthingham, which is said to have been the home of the descendents of Hacberd. Similarly Grainthorpe was believed to have been the village of a man named Geirmundr.

The study of place names is a complete project on its own, so will not be delved into further in this book, but it is a vast and fascinating subject to follow for those who are interested. It gives an insight into the history of our land, the peoples who dwelt there, the type of landscape which surrounded them and what importance they placed upon it. To try and view the land as it was in their times gives us a glimpse of what life was like for them and we begin to see how some of the folklore and legends originated.

Traditionally the capital of Lincolnshire, Lincoln, has a population of approximately 81,000 people. It was originally named Lindon, meaning 'the pool', as it was a settlement built by a deep pool along the River Witham. Later the Romans re-named it Lindum colonia, 'Roman colony', which eventually turned into what we now know as Lincoln. The city is teeming with history. One just has to walk down the main street to see how many interesting old buildings are left, without even mentioning the castle or the cathedral. The third largest in the country, the cathedral towers over the city, dominating the skyline. Legends abound around this colossal structure and ghost stories and folklore of the city are plentiful.

The county had a reputation for its wetlands and fens, as illustrated in this little ditty Mrs Gutch recorded for us for the early 1800s:

Cheshire for men,
Berkshire for dogs,
Bedfordshire for naked flesh,
And Lincolnshire for bogs.[13]

There is so much more, however, than the legendary boggy landscape. Described perfectly in *Brewer's Britain and Ireland*, Lincolnshire is:

...for the most part flat, and much of the south is taken up with the Fens, but it does manage to raise itself at least on to an elbow in two places, the Lincolnshire Edge (known locally as 'the Heights' or 'the Cliff'), a limestone escarpment running east to west on which the city of Lincoln is situated, and the Lincolnshire Wolds, a range of chalk hills running northeast-southwest in the eastern part of the county.[14]

And according to Jack Yates and Henry Thorold:

The landscape is of strongly contrasted kinds – one long and level with two-thirds of every eyeful sky. Wide and splendid cloudscapes and a great expanse of stars at night…The other sort of scenery is hilly, the rolling country of the Wolds, which seem very high by contrast but never rise more than 550 feet and

The long drainage ditches and narrow roads so characteristic of Lincolnshire.

are like the Downs, with beech plantations on their slopes and villages in their hollows and at their feet.[15]

Well known for its farming, Lincolnshire is 'overwhelmingly agricultural... the county supplies Britain with a cornucopia of vegetable...its pigs are famous...Lincolnshire sausages...'

Cumbrian and Lincolnshire sausages are two of the best known in the country but there were other farming traditions which made Lincolnshire famous. There is a specific Lincolnshire breed of sheep called Lincoln Longwool, larger and heavier than the Leicester, and also there is the Lincoln Red; a breed of red shorthorn beef and dairy cattle. There was once a breed of pig, the Lincolnshire Curly Coat, aptly named due to its woolly coat, but it has now died out.

Also known for its tremendous fishing industry, the Lincolnshire sailors and their wives have a tale or two to tell about life with the sea.

We shall begin our journey through Lincolnshire's store of tales and folklore by introducing the canny nature of the Lincolnshire folk through their shrewd tradition of decoy ducks.[16]

A community heavily reliant on agriculture, much of the Lincolnshire landscape encompasses fields upon fields of farmland.

They say that some Lincolnshire farmers used to breed ducks in a special way, for the specific purpose of betraying their fellow ducks! One source suggests there were up to forty such farms in the county, taking somewhere in the region of 13,000 birds via this method, in one season.

The decoy ducks were bred in specially designed ponds, where they were given much attention and care so that they became tame and fed from the farmer's hand. When they were ready they were 'sent' abroad, possibly to Europe, where they met other ducks and enticed them back to Lincolnshire, in their ducky language, with tales of a wondrous life!

When the decoy ducks returned with flocks of followers, the men began to secretly feed the newcomers handfuls of grain in the shallows of the ponds. The decoy ducks were used to this and happily went to eat and soon their new friends copied, confident in their host's judgement.

The grain was soon scattered in a wide open place and the ducks went there to eat it. Then it appeared in a narrower area, where the trees hung over like a tent. All the ducks now followed the food, feeling secure but unaware that there had been a large net placed in the foliage above their heads.

The decoy ducks had led their new friends into the netted area and all were feeding greedily, oblivious to the nets gradually lowering down on them with one end nipping into a point.

Suddenly a dog was let out and came towards them barking ferociously. The ducks all attempted to fly away but the net prevented their escape. They were instead driven towards the narrow point of the net where a man was waiting to catch them, one by one.

The decoy ducks were also caught but their fate was not the same as their new companions. They were stroked, calmed and placed back into a safe pond with plenty of food, ready for another flight to Europe. As for the foreign visitors, let us just hope the folk of Lincolnshire are kinder to people than ducks!

# 1

# THE DEVIL AND HIS SERPENT

Fables about the Devil abound all over the British Isles, and Lincolnshire is no exception. Superstition in Lincolnshire would not allow people to use his name: 'Don't say the Devil. Say the Owd Lad or he'll come when he's called.'[1]

Ethel Rudkin confirms this notion,[2] noting how he goes by many names in Lincolnshire, such as Old Nick, Old Sam, Sammiwell, Old Harry, the Old 'Un or Old Lad. However, even if he is not referred to directly, his appearances all over Lincolnshire are still rife – or maybe it is because of his regular visits that people try not to attract his attention!

Of course, there are exceptions to the rule and some people like courting trouble. It was believed by such folk that if you were to drop a pin in the keyhole of a church door and then run around the church seven times that the Devil would appear. Quite what they would do then is unclear.

The legend of Dorrington Church boasts a similar belief. On a clear, moon-lit night you can peek through the keyhole to watch the Devil playing with glass marbles across the church floor.

Exactly what Old Nick looks like we are not sure, although there is one story, retold by Rudkin,[3] that describes him as a 'funny little ole man'. He appeared when a young girl at Crosby decided she wanted to become a witch, and so at midnight one time she visited an old woman known locally as a witch. The old woman told the girl that, in order to become one, she must stand up then bend over and touch her toes, saying 'all that I 'ave a-tween me finger tips an' me toes I give to thee' (meaning the Devil). So the girl did as instructed, but just as she was half-way through her sentence, 'She see'd a funny little ole man come in an' sit i' th' chair opposite to 'er.' This figure frightened the girl,

A pub sign in Horncastle, an example of the Lincolnshire tradition of never naming the Devil directly.

who suddenly ended the sentence with 'I give to – Almighty God!' instead of the Devil. 'Well! – there was a ter-do-ment! The little ole man disappeared in a 'urry, an' th' owd woman was fit ter kill that lass, an' she was very glad ter escape out th' ouse.'

Folklorists Gutch and Peacock[4] relate a tradition used in Lincolnshire to have power over the Devil. They say on St Mark's Eve at midnight to hold two pewter platters under bracken for the seeds to drop into. The seed will go right through one and be caught in the other held below, whereupon the Devil will appear riding upon a pig and tell you anything you wish to know.

It is upon a huge black pig that the Devil will appear, again on St Mark's Eve, at Willoughton, but bizarrely only if you attempt to stop the horses and sheep which apparently kneel down and talk on this night. Legend states that whilst waiting in the stables some men did try this, but just before the appointed hour (always midnight) a mighty wind blew open the stable doors with a tremendous bang, whereupon the men fled home, terrified.

Also, a sure way to escape the contract if you have sold your soul to the Old Lad is to say he can amass the debt either inside the house, or outside. Then when the payment time comes, sit astride a windowsill or doorframe and he cannot collect.

If you wanted to see him, he is said to appear when he hears the clock strike twelve at The Devil's Pulpit stone in Tealby. He is supposed to come down to the stream for a drink. The only problem is you could be waiting a long while, as who knows when the Devil hears the clock strike here?

The church keyhole at Dorrington, through which one can observe the Devil playing marbles across the floor at night.

There is another Devil's Pulpit in Hemswell – a slab of rock that juts out above the natural spring. At the bottom of the hill here there is another stone which, legend states, children used to visit. They would apparently stick little pins into the holes in the rock, run round and round it very fast, then put their ears to the stone, and allegedly hear the Devil talking. One can understand this practice when observing the stone, as it is an unusual spherical shape.

The most well-known story of the Devil in Lincolnshire has to be connected to Lincoln Cathedral. A carving of him, peering over a witch's shoulder, can be seen high upon the side of the cathedral. This image gives credence to the old saying, 'He looks as the Devil over Lincoln'.[5] This particular phrase, used when one is jealous or has malicious intent, is said to derive from the displeasure of the Devil when the cathedral was built:

> The Devil is the map of malice, and his envy, as God's mercy, is over all his works. It grieves him whatever is given to God, crying out with that flesh devil, 'Ut quid hæc perditio' (what needs this waste?). On which account he is supposed to have overlooked this church, when first finished with a torve and tetric countenance, as maligning men's costly devotion, and that they should be so expensive in God's service.[6]

So annoyed was he at the completion of the building that legend states he decided to pay it a visit with his two little imp friends and have some fun.

> I'll blow up the chapter, and blow up the Dean;
> The canons I'll cannon right over the screen;
> I'll blow up the singers, bass tenor and boy;
> And the blower himself shall a blowing enjoy;

The Devil's Pulpit or Chair, situated on private land at the bottom of Beckhill Road, Tealby.

The Devil's Pulpit in Hemswell. Across a field and up a hill from Brook Street, this juts out of the cliff face, above three small springs.

Spherical rock just below the Devil's Pulpit stone at Hemswell. A spring runs out around the rock.

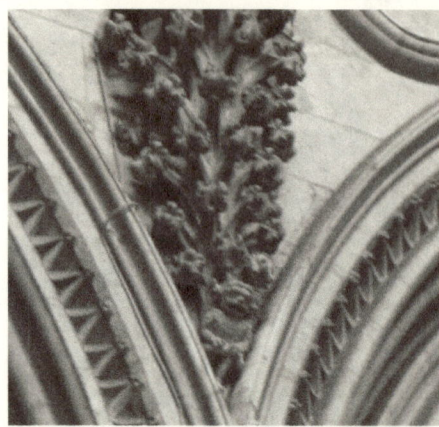

The Lincoln Imp, located in Lincoln Cathedral's Angel Choir, high up on the last but one column.

> The organist, too, shall right speedily find
> That I'll go one better in raising the wind;
> I'll blow out the windows, and blow out the lights,
> Tear vestments to tatters, put ritual to rights![7]

The imps entered the cathedral and began to cause chaos, tearing down tapestries, knocking over pews, pushing the bishop around and generally being very unpleasant and unruly – until an angel appeared and ordered them to stop. Of course they did not stop but carried on with their havoc until the angel had no choice but to make them stop. Just as one imp was throwing a rock at the angel, he was suddenly turned to stone in his tracks. The other, horrified, escaped and left the cathedral well alone but the petrified imp still stays in the cathedral as a reminder that the Devil should not toy with God's work!

> For the tiniest angel, with amethyst eyes
> And hair spun like gold, 'fore the alter did rise,
> Pronouncing these words in a dignified tone
> 'O impious Imp, be ye turned to stone!'

The petrified imp has become something of an attraction now, with tourists clamouring to get a glimpse of his cross-legged pose and wicked grin, peering down from his high place in the Angel Choir at the east end of the cathedral.

The Devil must have been a regular visitor to the cathedral, as there is a legend connected to the tomb of St Hugh. The belief was that when you closed your eyes to pray, you were in danger of the Devil coming up behind you, unseen, and so when you knelt to pray at St Hugh's shrine there was a shallow dip containing salt which you could take and throw over your left shoulder to blind his approach! This may have been the origin of the superstition that if one spills some salt accidentally, a pinch of it should be thrown over the left shoulder to blind the Devil.

Also, outside near the Chapter House there once stood a well and the myth ran that on Halloween, if you circled around it three times anticlockwise and then peered into its depths through holes in the walls, you would see the Devil.

Another popular visitation from the Devil appears in the form of wind. The *Lincolnshire Life* magazine explains that the residents of Boston have a special name for the footpath which runs between the river and the tower of Boston Stump.[8] They call it 'Windy Corner' and it seems that in this particular spot there is a constant wind. Even on a calm day there is a 'stiff breeze which seems to blow from all directions at once'. The legend states that St Botolph, to whom the church is dedicated, had an encounter with Old Nick here. They were engaged in an epic battle but Botolph came out victorious, giving the Devil such a beating that he is there, panting from exhaustion, or anger, to this very day.

A close-up carving depicting the Lincoln Imp. Found in the top Humber Bridge car park area, on the Hull side.

St Hugh's shrine is situated at the east end of the Angel Choir of Lincoln Cathedral, to the north side of the area below the great east window. A shallow depression a little to the left and behind the shrine is where the salt could have been kept.

They say that the buffeting gusts of wind that howl round the south-west side of Lincoln Cathedral are remnants of the great wind that threw back the Devil! This is an alternative version to the Lincoln Imp story – the Devil with a horde of demons came to cause havoc to the beautiful building in 1092. They swirled round the cathedral, intending to lay waste to it but the bishop, Remigius, prayed to the Virgin Mary for aid in defeating these foul beasts. His prayer was answered by a tremendous gust of wind, and the strength of it blew back the devilish crowd, defeating the Old 'Un and his cronies. However, legend tells that one imp was actually blown inside the cathedral but the stone angels protected their domain by petrifying the imp – hence the stone figure we see today.

These stories and the figure of the imp are so well known that today Lincoln City football team are nicknamed The Imps and the little Devil appears on their crest!

Adrian Grey has a variation on why this corner of the cathedral is so windy.[9] He says it was in the days when Lincoln fell into bad ways, with drunks and adulterers roaming the city. The Dean was apparently no better and was actually on good terms with the Devil. One day the Devil was visiting Lincolnshire with his friend, the wind, causing a bit of a stir and blowing up trouble, when he looked upon Lincoln and decided to pop in and see the Dean.

They made their way to the cathedral but the Devil told the wind to wait outside for him. The wind waited and waited, blustering around but the Devil never returned and so the wind waits there still.

The *Lincolnshire Life* magazine tells us of an incident when an angel disrupted another of the Devil's plans.[10] A rich squire named Simon Greenleaf, who owned Nut Hall, Quadring, refused to give alms to the village church, as expected from a man of his standing. His loyalties lay elsewhere and it is said he practised black magic in the tower of his residence. The local priest was irritating him and they had had a few arguments, one of which left Greenleaf with the desire for revenge. Using his black magic he brewed up a potion 'which would destroy the souls of the infants which it touched'. He broke into the church and swapped the font water for his devilish creation, knowing there was to be a christening the next day. Little did he realise, however, that he was being observed – an angel appeared and commanded him to leave. In his irreverence, he taunted and laughed at the angel who then took up the font and poured the evil mixture all over Greenleaf. He ran from the church screaming and when people came to see what was going on, they found him stone dead in the graveyard.

The Devil is often blamed for people's misdemeanours, unfortunate events or bad luck. One old belief in Lincolnshire was that every Michaelmas night the Devil would travel around and spit on all the blackberries, and so after this date they were not fit to be eaten. Michaelmas occurs on 29 September, which is naturally towards the end of the blackberry season – a convenient tale to explain their decay. Gutch and Peacock add that when Satan was thrown out of heaven he fell into a bramble bush and was sorely annoyed![11] Thus every year he spoils the very bushes that remind him of his fall and the berries become 'as hard as the Devil's forehead'.

Rudkin quotes a Mr Sibsey, who tells of another old belief that helps to explain the supposed power Old Nick has over crops:

> In the neighbourhood of Frieston, triangular corners of fields are filled with trees, and the groups were known as 'Devil's Holts'. The belief is still current that these were left for the Devil to play in, otherwise he would play in the fields and spoil the crops.

Polly Howat relates an interesting story of the unfortunate farmer John Leech, who got on the wrong side of the Devil.[12] The legend says Leech was rather the worse for wear in his local tavern and his friend wanted him to go home. Leech, however, wanted to stay and apparently shouted, 'Let the Devil take him who goeth out of this house today,' and they both carried on drinking. Eventually Leech decided to leave, as he wanted to go to the local Whittlesey Fair, near Raveley. His friend was said to remind him of the oath he swore, but the farmer just laughed and started his journey. He was so drunk, however, that he lost his way and ended up riding round in circles until nightfall. Two griffins then appeared and barred

What is left of the Melton Ross gallows today, in a field next to a lay-by along the A18, midway between Melton Ross and Wrawby.

the poor man's way and he heard a dreadful voice remind him of the oath he had broken. Leech was terrified and fell from his horse, whereupon two imps emerged from the bushes and began to beat him. They hauled him up into the sky and flew with him for miles, eventually dropping him and disappearing. The blood stained farmer was found the next morning and taken to a local house, where a doctor was called. The poor man seemed to have lost his mind and tried to attack the parson, who was summoned after he had narrated his tale. The frightened locals tied him to the bed and locked his door overnight. All seemed very quiet in the morning, so they unlocked the door, but were faced with a horrible sight. Leech's neck had been broken and his body was black and swollen all over, with every bone pulled out of joint. It was then that his story was believed and all who saw his body realised the awful consequences of making drunken oaths.

Rudkin tells the tale of another man, Tommy Lindrum, who sold his soul to the Devil. As the road was usually so bad between Wroot and Lindholme, he decided one day to make a causeway between the two. The Devil pledged to help his disciple, boasting he would make it faster than a man on a horse could gallop. For some reason, however, the Devil seemed to give up helping Tommy halfway through the job. It has been speculated that Tommy had tricked him somehow and thus escaped with his soul intact. People say there is still evidence of the beginnings of a cobbled causeway there now, although it is mostly grassed over. The legend states it is bad luck to touch the stones, and one farmer, when he tried to move them, lost all his horses in the process – they just dropped down dead!

Another well-known tale[13] is that of four boys who were playing at the site of the gallows at Melton Ross in the 1790s. With the thoughtlessness of youth they were playing at 'hanging', whereby each one would hang from the gallows with a noose around his neck for as long as possible, then his friends would lift him up and let him breathe again. One of the boys had just started hanging when an injured, three-legged hare was said to have limped past. This caught the attention of the other three who thought they could catch the poor thing. When they went to grab it, however, the hare suddenly ran off into the woods with the boys in hot pursuit, completely forgetting their friend. When they eventually returned after losing the hare in the undergrowth, their friend was dead. Belief was that the hare was in fact the Devil in disguise that fateful day. After all, it was surmised, the Devil is the epitome of evil and desires to destroy anything that is good and pure.

He was also said to have been seen frolicking round Church Hill at Dorrington one night as a white rabbit, before changing back into the figure of the Devil. Hares and rabbits seem to be a popular form of disguise for witches too, who are said to be the Devil's handmaidens.

Ghost story writer Polly Howat describes one incident where the Devil rescues a witch from an angry mob of locals intent on killing her. The witch was called Crazy Kate and apparently used to visit the Manwar Rings at Swineshead

Manwar Rings, an overgrown grass-topped plateau surrounded by a deep moat, can be found across a farmer's field over the road in a westerly direction from the old Swineshead Abbey House. Thought to be an old Danish encampment and the resting place of Hubba the Dane, it was also used in the Second World War as an ammunitions depository. Traces of this can still be found in the undergrowth.

to commune with her master. There were many unfortunate happenings in the village at that time and the locals began to suspect Kate, especially as she had three cats, which are well known witch familiars. They gave her an ultimatum, to leave town or have her house burnt down, but Kate allegedly cursed them and promised misfortune to any who tried to harm her. More misfortune befell the village and when a baby died there was uproar, even the priest blamed Kate and said more children would die if something was not done. The mob needed no further encouragement and went to Kate's house to kill her, but she was not there. Eventually they tracked her to Manwar Rings, where she was standing on top of the bank. Just as they were closing in on her, 'A black cloaked stranger rode up the mound on a powerful black foam-lathered horse, whose hooves thundered and echoed around the encampment.'[14] This devilish figure swept her away and she was never seen again.

Thoughout history, the Devil seems to know when there are any actions being performed that display human weakness. His evil radar is alerted and he swoops in to help continue the chaos and corruption. One example of this in Lincolnshire was around 869 at the Benedictine abbey at Crowland. The legend goes that the monks had fallen into sinful ways, drinking heavily and behaving in a manner unbefitting their order. It was rumoured that one monk had even sold his soul to Satan, for the secret of everlasting life. One day, after months of dreadful behaviour, there was a terrible rumbling of thunder which shook the very walls of the monastery.

The ruins of Crowland Abbey, Peterborough, with the parish church fully intact behind.

Trinity Bridge, Crowland, is another ancient monument worth a look whilst in the town. The wooden version of the structure was first mentioned in a charter of King Edred in 943, and the present stone bridge dates from the fourteenth century. It is an amazing structure, reminding us of the great changes to the surrounding landscape, as there is no water to be seen now. An interesting statue resides there, thought to be either Christ or King Ethelbald.

A terrifying black cloud grew around the building from which a great figure could be seen to emerge. 'It was Satan himself ... so fearful in countenance, so diabolical in its malignity that all fell cowering before the vision.'[15]

It seems that he had been sent to them by God, who was so appalled at their behaviour that he had left them in the Devil's hands. He told them they were cursed and that within twelve months the abbey would be in ruins. The monks were terrified that they would be damned for all eternity and vowed to be more reverent, but as the months passed and the horror of that night faded from their memories, they began to slip back into their old ways.

Then one day the monk on lookout saw something in the distance that made the memory come back with full force. He relayed the news to the others and eventually they could all make out the fleet of Viking longboats approaching. The monks fled to the chapel and prayed for deliverance but each could hear the Devil's knowing laugh reverberating through their heads.

The Vikings were merciless and slaughtered as many of the monks as they could find, ransacking the abbey and pillaging whatever they could lay their hands on. There was nothing left when they had finished, just as the Devil had predicted, save for a pile of corpses that they set fire to.

Often when talking of the Devil, dragons are included in the stories. Dragons are age-old mythological creatures that predate any history we have.

A depiction of the King's Lynn coat of arms.

Whether legend or fact, they have populated stories in every culture throughout time. China uses the symbol of the dragon in much of its mythology as representing strength and power, whereas in western culture dragons are viewed as evil creatures, often connected to the Devil – apart from Wales, which is proud of its dragon connections.

> And war broke out in heaven. Michael and his angels fought against the dragon. The dragon and his angels fought back, but they were defeated, and there was no longer any place for them in heaven. The great dragon was thrown down, that ancient serpent, who is called the Devil and Satan, the deceiver of the whole world – he was thrown down to the earth, and his angels were thrown down with him.[16]

The arms of King's Lynn, Norfolk, depict a dragon's head pierced by a cross. The legend behind this involves St Margaret of Antioch, a noble virgin-martyr whom the Devil devoured whilst in the form of a dragon, but the faithful child always wore a cross around her neck and by its power she was able to burst the dragon open and escape, unhurt.

Treasure is also factored into many local dragon tales, such as the two serpents that guard Cissbury Ring, an Iron Age hill fort, where a wealth of gold and gems is supposedly buried. Also the legend that a flying dragon may still pass overhead between Devon's Dolbury Hill and Cadbury Hill, guarding each location where it hid riches, and the story of a worm which abides at Gunnarton Castle, also known as Money Hill due to the legends of treasure in the area.

Turning our attention back to Lincolnshire, there are two boulders of Spilsby sandstone which sit outside the south gateway of St Edith's Church, known as the Drake Stone. Some folklorists believe 'drake' to be a corruption of 'dragon'. The Drake Stone, always referred to in the singular, has various stories attached to it, including variations as to why it is named thus.

Folklorist Ethel Rudkin quotes from one traditional account of the stones that she found which referred to them as the 'Duck and Drake Stones'.[17] She goes on to explain that Duckstone was a popular Lincolnshire game at the end of the nineteenth century, which may have given name to these stones, but she thinks actually that Drake is being used in the same sense as the expression 'fire drake'.

In Germanic mythology a fire drake was a fire-breathing dragon with a reptilian body and sometimes also with wings. In these German and also Celtic myths the fire drake often lived in caves and guarded some great treasure.

The story here runs that a local man was ploughing his field, which was known as 'Drake Stone Close', when suddenly his horses and plough started disappearing into what seemed like quicksand. He tried with all his might to wrench his horses out of danger, whilst keeping himself on firm ground, but they were steadily sucked under until they disappeared completely. Then, startling the poor man even more, a creature suddenly flew out of the hole and rose into the sky, quacking!

This is where the story breaks into two camps. One camp claims it was a drake which flew from the hole, the other of course asserts it was a dragon which flew from the hole, where lay the treasure that it had been guarding.

Rudkin declares that the farmer returned to the site of the incident the very next day, but the ground was completely firm. There was, however, a large

A stained-glass window at St Margaret's Church, King's Lynn, showing St Margaret of Antioch defeating the dragon.

The Drake Stone's final resting place, outside St Edith's Church, Anwick.

boulder on the spot, which resembled something like a drake's head, hence the name Drake Stone. Again, we are unsure as to whether this was the bird or a dragon and as the stone has broken into two pieces, it is difficult now to see any shape resembling either. The latter seems perhaps more convincing, especially as the village of Dragonby, near Scunthorpe, is named after a natural outcrop of rock which looks like a dragon.

Naturally, after this event many people tried their hand at retrieving the treasure buried beneath the stone, though none were successful. One man, it is said, chose some particularly strong oxen to help move the boulder, to which he fastened great chains, but even though they pulled with all their might they only managed to move it an inch before the chains broke and the oxen collapsed, exhausted. Then the drake or dragon made another appearance – flying out from under the stone, surveying the scene and then returning to its guardian position.

After that it was left alone for a while, but it began to annoy the farmer, who constantly had to plough around it when working in his field. Eventually he had a large hole dug next to it and, presumably with the greatest of difficulty, had the boulder rolled in. Rudkin tells us that it was one Reverend Dodsworth, then vicar of Anwick, who didn't want the stone to be lost, so commissioned a traction engine to haul it to its present place beside the church.

She finishes by quoting a parishioner of Anwick, from 1931, who stated the Drake Stone came to be thus named because when men went to work in the mornings they would always see two drakes sheltering beneath it. In this instance we should presume drake refers to the bird and not the dragon, and it was such a common sight that the stone became known as the Drake Stone because of it. According to legend, the stone broke into the two parts we now see when it was moved from the field. As for the treasure, it was never known to be found and so one can only assume the dragon guards it still, or some very feisty ducks!

There is a boulder at Winceby near an area locally known as Slash Hollow, where there is also said to be buried treasure. The legend states that any attempt to move the large stone always failed, and on one occasion a farmer made a great effort with horses and chains. It was said the stone actually began to move and one of the men helping the farmer was supposed to have said 'Let God or the Devil come now for we have it!'[18] at which point a figure appeared, standing on the stone. It was the Devil himself, as summoned, and he left his claw mark in the rock, which can still be seen today. Of course, the men let the stone drop and no one tried again for a long time, knowing the Devil himself was guarding this treasure. The locals are actually said to call it Devil's Stone and other attempts to move it in the future saw a black mouse run out and frighten the horses away from the stone for good.

The field here was the site of a terrible battle during the English Civil War and the soldiers would sharpen their blades on the stone. It is said that Slash Hollow ran ankle deep in blood that fateful day as so many were slaughtered, and one legend believes the bodies of the soldiers were buried under the stone with treasure and riches that had been looted – perhaps explaining the presence of Old Nick.

The Winceby Slash Stone, at the side of the road along Slash Lane, the B1195, between Horncastle and Spilsby.

The tale of the dragon of Castle Carlton, near Louth, is considerably more detailed than the Anwick tale, with no confusion as to what the beast was. The story runs that one Sir Hugh Barde, in the first year he came into the baronetcy, fought the dragon of Castle Carlton, whose people were being terrorised by a 'dragon in a lane in the field that venomed men and bestes with his aire'.[19]

Marlow describes it as a mighty beast, with a 'long scaly body, short iron-shod legs, lashing tail, and head, in which was set one blazing eye the size of a basin'.[20] It was the terror of the countryside, causing chaos and devastation, devouring anyone it could get its teeth into. Its very breath was poison and even more deadly than the flames it exhaled. The scaly hide was so thick it seemed impenetrable and the people despaired, believing that they would never be able to overcome it.

The beast had one spot, however, that was vulnerable; a protruding wart on its right thigh that, if pierced, would kill the dragon outright. It guarded this area well and it seemed the beast never slept and so could not be caught off guard.

The idea of a dragon having a vulnerable spot is a common theme in dragon lore. Ralph Whitlock is something of a dragon expert and likens the Castle Carlton dragon to the Wantley dragon, which had a vulnerable place in the middle of its back and a dragon at Newcastle whose vulnerable spot was its navel.

Sir Hugh made a pledge to the people that he would slay the Castle Carlton dragon whatever it took, and would take its head to the king. He chose a wedding day, which portended good luck and set out with his sword and shield to hunt the beast down. He found it resting on the beach, after a hearty dinner of seven servants from the castle. Although it seemed asleep, 'the cunning creature's eye was ever vigilant. The dragon lay quietly but alert, waiting for its moment to strike.'[21]

The brave knight suddenly cried out to St Bartholomew and St Guthlac to aid him in his quest, and as he was praying he heard an answer surround him, a booming voice, which told him, 'Look for the bright light from heaven which shall blind the dragon – in the instant that light shines, strike hard or thou must perish'.

At this the dragon rose from its slumber, spreading its wings and flying straight towards its prey with the swiftness of a falcon. At that very moment the sky turned black and a sudden downpour descended in a torrent between Sir Hugh and the dragon. There was a tremendous rumble as thunder shook the sky and then a sudden blinding flash of lightning split the air, illuminating the dragon in all its terrible glory – shining directly upon the exposed wart. Sir Hugh took his opportunity and lifted his great sword, striking down with all his might to cleave the vulnerable mark. The mighty monster's screech was equal to that of the thunderous storm raging all around them and it was so enraged that it sought to kill Sir Hugh with a vengeance. The saints were still helping him, however, and the dragon became lost and disorientated in the thick clouds billowing around them. All the while its life force was draining away, bleeding out of the fatal wound in its thigh. Eventually the beast dropped onto the sand, defeated, and the clouds cleared to show the prostrate form of the dead dragon lying at Sir Hugh's feet. With one deft stroke, he sliced the head off and carried it back to the village to announce his victory. The people rejoiced at their freedom from that mighty terror and Sir Hugh became a hero.

As promised, he took the dragon's head to King Henry I. The king changed Hugh's name to Bardolph and as Castle Carlton was the head of the baronetcy, he granted it many privileges, such as freedom from all tolls for Sir Hugh's tenants and the right to take a horn of salt from every salt cart passing through his domain. Sir Hugh did not forget the help he had been given and made a pilgrimage to the saints' shrine to lay down treasures and thanks. His deed was talked of widely, as was his bravery and the privileges he bestowed upon his people. *The Lincolnshire Magazine* states that it was 'this same valiant knight [who] had lands in Norfolk, his chief seat there being Wormgay, which name again retains the "dragon" tradition'.

Perhaps he and his ancestors were old hands at confronting dragons. It seems the baron's crest included the image of a dragon's head, but when researching Wormgay, the village's name seems to stem from a family or the followers of a man called Wyrma. I can find no dragon legend attached to the area. Adrian Gray[22] suggests the Castle Carlton dragon may have lived at Walmsgate, near Louth, but that it was then known as Wormsegay. There is a long barrow at Walmsgate, which legend states holds the skeleton of a dragon that was slain in the area. If it is headless, then perhaps we would find our answer.

Whitlock quotes from a very early source, William Camden, writing in 1586:

Sir Hugh Bardolfe lived in Castle Carlton in the time of Henry I. It is said in a very old court roll that in the first year that Sir Hugh was lord of the place ther reigned at a toune called Wormesgay a dragon in a lane in a field that venomed men and bestes with his aire; Sir Hugh on a weddings day did fight with thys dragon and slew him, and toke his head, and beare it to the kynge and gave it him, and the kynge for slaying of the dragon put to his name this word dolfe, and did calle him afterwards Bardolfe; for it was before Sir Hugh Barde; and the kynge gave hym in his armes then a dragon in sygne.[23]

In old Germanic *dolph* means 'famous wolf' – which could be a champion's title given for bravery. Whitlock also proposes that Walmsgate may have originally been named Wormsgate.

Folklorists Gutch and Peacock refer to 'a tradition, which probably took its rise at an early period, [which] tells of a huge serpent that devastated the village of South Ormsby and was slain at the adjacent hamlet of Walmsgate.'[24] This could be either another version of the slaying of the dragon and its burial in the barrow, or the tale of a different dragon, making the area rather unlucky in this respect! One version does suggest that there were actually three dragons in the area; one buried in the barrow, one flying away to settle in Dragon's Hole in Corringham Scroggs, and the third fatally wounded, crawling away to die at Ormsby.

Gutch and Peacock state that *ormr* was the old Norse form of Anglo-Saxon *wyrm*, and in dragon tradition worm was another name for dragon, just like drake.

In many stories of dragons they are depicted as worm-like creatures, with no wings – like the famous Lambton Worm, a legend from the North East of England. South Ormsby, therefore, was apparently named after the dragon incident, as was, we assume, Walmsgate.

The worm-like dragons have also been depicted as serpents – and through much of history they have been linked with water: 'On that day the Lord with his cruel and great and strong sword will punish Leviathan the fleeing serpent, Leviathan the twisting serpent; and he will kill the dragon that is in the sea.'[25] In fact, it is said the English word dragon derives from the Greek *drakon*, meaning serpent of huge size/water snake.

There is another tale of a defeated dragon in Lincolnshire, at Buslingthorpe, near Lincoln. The famous dragon-slayer in this instance was Sir Buslingthorpe, who died around 1250. An effigy of this knight is housed in the little church of Buslingthorpe, St Michael's. He was thought to have attacked the ferocious dragon and killed it and for such bravery and prowess, Sir John was awarded 400 acres of local land, known as Lissington Pasture. *The Lincolnshire Magazine* suggests that he actually drained and reclaimed this marshy land, making it habitable, and this was how his fame arose.

The effigy of Sir Buslingthorpe inside the small church, aptly named St Michael's, at Buslingthorpe. The church is one of the few remaining buildings on the site of a deserted medieval village. The tower is all that survives from medieval times, the rest having being rebuilt in 1835, but the whole structure overlies the buried remains of a much older church.

# THE DEVIL AND HIS SERPENT 39

The head of the dragon-shaped rock residing on the hillside in the small village of Dragonby. Halfway down the road through the village there is a gap in the houses on the right-hand side. A track leads onto some open ground and the dragon can be clearly seen winding its way down the hill on the right, as if heading to drink from the pond at the bottom.

Part of the tail of the colossal stone dragon at Dragonby.

The fact that boggy, watery land was involved, however, seems to agree with the alleged link to serpents and worm-like dragons.

The other dragon we briefly touched on earlier was the creature that lived at Dragonby. The legend states this beast was the guardian of some mines but was defeated by a wizard, who turned it to stone – hence the ninety foot dragon-shaped rock that can be seen snaking its way up the hillside. It is actually a natural rock formation, apparently caused by a limestone spring, but legends often attach themselves to such wonders of nature. This particular rock has another myth attached to it, one concerning the Devil. The tale states that the 'dragon' rock is in fact the top of a church that once stood there but sank into the ground, congregation and all – and once a year the ghostly bells can still be heard to ring. The Devil had been attracted to the village because, as Daniel Codd tells us, 'The community had fallen into avaricious ways.'[26]

He caused the church to sink and sat on the roof, laughing all the while. When the congregation tried to leave they found themselves in a long, underground tunnel which led only down, to Hell!

# 2

# THE WET AND WILDS

When thinking of Lincolnshire, picturing the extensive North Sea coastline along one border, the boundaries of the River Trent and the Humber, and the endless horizon viewed over the miles of open countryside, one inevitably imagines vast expanses of low-lying wetlands, fens and marshes. The magnificent Lincolnshire Wolds and heathland stand tall amongst the peat and silt-filled depressions of the Fens and the salt-lined marshes. The fact is that forty per cent of Lincolnshire's land is at or below sea level, three quarters of the land lying below thirty metres. This is one of the reasons why, for many years, the Fenland was a very isolated place, difficult to get to and then hard to traverse, and so strangers mostly stayed away. It is little wonder that in such out-of-the-way places legends and folk tales arose, mingled with the history of the area, abounding with stories of strange creatures, especially those lurking in the wet and wilds! Before the eighth century, Lincolnshire was apparently described as 'a deep and horrible fen, a strange land of fetid pools and flowing rivers, and a terrain grim enough to daunt all but the most intrepid settler.'[1] The chronicler Felix of Crowland is said to have described it as, 'A trackless waste of immense marshes and foul running streams…oft-times clouded with moist and dark vapours…the haunt of the Devil.'[2]

Despite its reputation as an inhospitable wet and marshy area, Lincolnshire also had many scholars defending it. In the *Lincolnshire Bedside Book*, Jack Yates and Henry Thorold are quoted explaining the difference between the Marsh and the Fens:

> The Marsh is the low land of narrow dykes, meres and pools which stretches along the sea coast between the wash and the Humber. The east wind constantly

An example of what the fens could have looked like in the eighth century, although now so well drained and managed that the land would be unrecognisable to the people of that era.

blows over it from the North Sea, the water in the dykes is brackish with salt that has percolated through the sand. These are areas of rich pasture land, stiff grass and wild fowl. The Fen is not salt, nor is it near the sea except in small patches. Most of it is drained silt-land, ditched and dried out to produce rich cornland and fields for bulbs and flowers.[3]

Ten thousand years ago, at the end of the most recent glacial period, Britain was joined to Europe via a Dutch province and the area around Norfolk. It is thought, from studies of the bed of the North Sea, that rivers in the southern part of eastern England flowed into the River Rhine and through the English Channel. From the Fens northwards, the drainage flowed into the northern part of the North Sea and when the ice melted, the rising sea level flooded the lower-level lands, including the Fenland basin, which had previously been dense woodland. This gradually led to the extensive salt and freshwater wetlands Jack Yates and Henry Thorold describe.

Christopher Marlow relates an interesting alternate myth about how the Lincolnshire Fenlands were created. The story is set during the time of the Roman occupation, under the rule of the governor Valerian. Legend says that it was the Iceni tribe who suffered under his terrible rule and his treatment of them was vicious and callous. He would hack off prisoners' ears and noses just for his amusement and then let them loose in the woods, only to be hunted down by savage dogs.

However, he apparently went too far when he captured the local priest's daughter, Rowena. She was known throughout the district for her beauty and the Iceni were extremely angry when they heard she was being used as Valerian's play thing. Rowena's father, Mandru, called for a meeting of fellow priests at the temple of the sea god, and many of the oppressed tribesmen attended. All present had grievances with the Romans, and all were in favour when Mandru suggested a rebellion. Unfortunately, however, their meeting was stormed by Roman guards who killed many, and seven priests, including Mandru, were taken to Valerian's palace and tortured. Luckily, Mandru managed to escape but his six companions were hung on crosses to die. Mandru wept bitterly for his fellow priests and that day he swore an oath that he would help his people. He was not seen for some time but a few months later a stranger came to the area. He visited the streets of the town and whenever he came across a British Iceni slave he whispered a warning to them: 'Friend, arise this night and be gone. Destruction comes fast upon this city and if thou tarry, there shall be no escape.'[4]

On hearing this old man's warning, many of the Iceni took heed and packed up their belongings ready to steal away in the middle of the night. Then, some time during the night, a sudden and ferocious wind blew in from the sea. It blew open the gates of the city and as every Roman was asleep, the way to escape was made clear for the British slaves. The Iceni gasped in amazement and crept out stealthily, so as not to wake the guards. When they made it to the woods, they met up with other tribes from nearby towns who had also had the warning from the mysterious stranger. As they were talking and exchanging stories, the stranger himself appeared among them and to everyone's astonishment they discovered it was Mandru, bidding them to listen to him: 'There is no time to delay – the gods are angry with Rome and intend to destroy every Roman city. It has been revealed to me where I shall lead you, but delay not or we shall all be lost.' He then led them far away to the high ground.

When dawn broke, the Romans awoke and were baffled by the forceful winds blowing around the city, and then they discovered the gates were wide open and the slaves had all escaped. They were furious but the force of the tempest now raging round them prevented them tracking down the escapees. The soldiers became even more enraged when Valerian ordered them to do all those tasks commonly allotted to the slaves.

As the day progressed, a curious cloud-like phenomenon was observed over the sea. The Romans flocked to try and see what it was but no one could make it out. The longer they watched, however, the more the strange mass seemed to resemble a huge column of water, rising higher and higher out of the sea as it came closer and closer. Then a messenger came from the shore to tell of a mountain of water rushing towards the town. Everyone dashed outside to look and '…in truth the column appeared at the very least 300 feet high, and seemed as if all the ocean were gathered up into it.'

The terrified Romans fled into the forest where they met other Romans from other cities, who were also trying to escape the menacing torrent. There was no escape, however, and the colossal waves crashed into the cities, destroying Valerian's palace as well as all the houses and streets. It swept away all traces of Roman supremacy and then it rushed through the forest, washing away all the trees and swallowing up the hills and rivers. High in the upland range, the Iceni watched the sea smash against the ground below them, obliterating everything in its path, but fortunately they were high enough up and the waves abated just below them, sparing their lives. They looked down in awe on what used to be thick forest and now appeared to be a huge inland sea, with small islands appearing here and there. The Iceni rejoiced and Mandru shouted out:

> We of the Iceni are the first to repeople the wilderness...and these parts shall never more become forest. The sea, our great deliverer, shall always be present here, in token whereof it has been decreed that we shall be known henceforth as Gyrvii or marsh-men, in place of Iceni, the slaves of the Romans.

This is the legend of how the Fens and marshland originated and the people who lived there became some of the best fishermen and wildfowlers that lived. Marlow does add that the Romans re-conquered the area but not to the extent that they had before the floods. Efforts to tame the Fens were attempted, with banks and roads winding their way through the area but it remained for centuries the haunt of fish and birds with many islands surrounded by marshy wetland.

Of course there is evidence to suggest that humans populated the area from the Mesolithic period, before the Iceni and the Roman times. The low-lying wetlands would have been seen as an advantageous area to live, hunting and fishing being vital activities for survival. Sources suggest the area was also favoured by warriors because it formed a naturally safe area. Their homes, surrounded by water, were easier to defend.

Around the fifth century, during the time of King Vortigern, the Saxons were given the Fenlands in Lincolnshire to inhabit. Hengist and his brother Horsa had asked Lord Vortigern to give them homes, as they had been exiled from Germany. Vortigern, thinking they were savages but could be useful for protection, gave them land in Lincolnshire. McLeish tells us that Vortigern hoped that the draining of the marshes and muddy fields and fens would use up all their energy and leave them no time to be a threat to him. One day Hengist asked if he could build a castle in Lincolnshire, '...as large as can be encircled by a single leather thong and let me invite more of my followers from Germany, enough to fill it'.[5]

Vortigern envisaged how short leather thongs were and thought it would be a tiny castle with just a small number of soldiers, and so gave permission. Jennifer Westwood quotes Abraham de la Pryme, describing the story in the 1600s:

> ...Hengist begg'd so much ground of King Vortigern as he was able to encompass with an ox-hide, who, not well understanding his meaning, granted him his request, thinking that he meant no more than he could cover with an ox-hide.

But Hengist cut it all into small thongs, and by that means encompast in round about a great compass of land, and built an exceeding strong castle upon part thereof, part of whose ruins I took notice of, it being a wall five or six yards thick. But, when Christianity came, they pull'd the castle down, and built the church in the place where it stood, of the stone that it was built off.[6]

McLeish explains how the thong was put to such good use:

At once Hengist slaughtered the largest bull in Lincolnshire, and set his butchers the task of slicing the hide into a continuous thong as thin as a woollen thread and over a kilometre long. He used it to measure out the land for a castle, and when the castle was built he brought from Germany eighteen long-ships filled with warriors, and with them his daughter, the witch, Renwein.

Renwein was very attractive and her hand in marriage was offered to Vortigern, in exchange for the county of Kent, including Vortigern's own castle. Vortigern fell under her spell and agreed not only to this but also to allow more warriors from Germany to inhabit the countryside around the Humber. The British people, however, were beginning to panic about the number of Saxons in the country and their loyalties switched to Vortigern's son, Vortimer. They gathered an army and attacked the Saxons, defeating them in four bloody battles. Hengist fled back to Germany and Vortimer went to visit his father and stepmother to discuss the future of Britain. The witch, Renwein, however, put poison in his goblet and he died a slow and painful death. Once Vortigern regained his power and was back on the throne, Renwein sent word to Hengist to return. This he did with many warriors and this time he won the battles and the Saxons ruled Britain, pillaging and destroying anything British, so the work of draining the Fens was never completed.

Thus, as Stewart Bennett tells us, travel through medieval Lincolnshire was very difficult because of the amount of water, making its relative isolation even more pronounced:

The only reasonable roads were those left by the Romans although, as they had been neglected for over 700 years, they had fallen into disrepair. Rivers were mostly navigable all year round, but roads were liable to floods in the winter only to dry out, causing deep ruts, in the summer. As much of the county was low-lying, travel in the Fens and marsh during winter months was at best difficult, and often impossible.[7]

The Lincolnshire wetlands were finally drained by Cornelius Vermuyden and his followers in the seventeenth century. The indigenous Carr people hated these Dutch intruders as they were taking away the livelihood of fowling and fishing, which they had been doing for so many generations. There were many murders during the draining days and the Carr people used the legend of the Tiddy Mun as an 'explanation' for the deaths.

Polly Howat relates the story of the 'Tiddy Mun Without a Name'. He was a creature who lived in waterholes in the Fens, only coming out at night. He had the appearance of an old man, with long white hair and a beard, but he was only the size of a small child. He wore grey so that he was difficult to see at dusk, his laugh sounded more like a screech and no one ever knew his name. He had a strange relationship with the people of the Fens, for although they were wary of him he would help them when the flood waters came. The people would call to him, 'Tiddy Mun, without a name, the water's rough!'[8]

In the morning the flood water would have gone, as the Tiddy Mun had taken it away, and they knew he would always be good to them as long as the Fens remained. However, with the influx of the Dutch and the draining work they were doing, local people were scared that bad times were ahead.

Then drainers began to disappear and word was that the Tiddy Mun had drowned them. More workers were brought in and they too were drowned, but after a while it wasn't just the Dutch drainers that were vanishing, the Tiddy Mun was angry with everyone for destroying his home. Children and animals succumbed to illness, crops failed and life started to go wrong for everyone. After much discussion the people agreed some water must be returned if the Tiddy Mun was to be appeased and so the locals took pans of water out on the night of the new moon and offered them to him, asking for a truce. They waited in silence for a long time until eventually they heard his screeching laugh and they knew they had forged a pact. For many years after this night, the local people offered the Tiddy Mun water at every new moon and peace was maintained.

Adrian Gray says that the Tiddy People were a race of strange creatures that lived in the wet and marshy areas. He agrees that they were very small, like children, or even babies, but with long thin arms and large feet. They reputedly had long noses and wide mouths with long tongues. Instead of grey, he believed they wore green coats, hence the nickname 'greencoaties', often with a yellow bonnet. The Tiddy Mun was similar to a tribal chief and Adrian Gray recounts a rhyme people apparently chanted in the Fen areas:

Tiddy Mun wi'out a name
White he'ad, walking la'ame
While the watter te'ems the Fen
Tiddy Mun'll harm nane.[9]

The Tiddy People were very useful for everyday life. It was they who would pinch the buds on the trees in spring to make them open and would paint the colours on the flowers every year. Farmers would leave small gifts for them so their crops would not be harmed and people thought it an honour if the Tiddy People came into their houses to warm themselves by the fire. They have hardly ever been seen though, since the draining of the Fens and all the trouble with the Dutch workers, so where they have found a suitable home is a mystery.

Will-o-the-Wisps, or Will-o-the-Wykes in Lincolnshire, also known as Jack-o-Lanterns, corpse candles or *ignis fatuus* in Latin, translating as 'foolish fire', are mysterious, ghostly wisps or lanterns of light, seen hovering over marshy lands, usually at twilight. Myth tells of strange fairies or ghosts of the dead creating these torches, although some scientific theories explain them as gases, produced by the organic decay in the wetlands, causing a glowing light. Of course, with such an eerie phenomenon, stories of these peculiar lights abound throughout folk lore, usually including legends of people being lured off the main path, following the lights, and never being seen again. The Lincolnshire Fens were one such place where these ethereal lights were seen, and warnings to stay away from them were whispered throughout communities.

These stories make similar appearances in many cultures around the globe. It has been said that in some Australian Aboriginal tribes, these eerie sightings were believed to be the spirits of lost or stillborn children. They called them the 'min-mim' and they were feared as dangerous creatures. Variations of the Tiddy Mun story in Lincolnshire say that when the people called to the Tiddy Mun appealing for mercy, they heard the wailings and whimpering of babies in the air and some even felt the cold embraces of their dead children, whom the Tiddy Mun had taken.

The Shag Foal is another beast that haunts Lincolnshire, leading travellers off the beaten path and into the marshes and bogs with its eyes blazing like beacons.

A stream found between Brigg and Wrawby, possibly where the Shag Foal was seen.

Some say it is one and the same as the Will-o-the-Wisps, others say it is a creature akin to a rough-coated donkey or foal. The unsuspecting travellers follow the lights of its eyes and then become stuck in the bogs, whereupon the creature shows itself with a hideous laugh, half human half animal. One well-known sighting of the Shag Foal was near a stream between Wrawby and Brigg. This beast was known as the Lackey Causey Calf and tried to lead people into the stream.

Folklorists Westwood and Simpson also mention the Lackey Causey Calf, claiming it is sometimes purported as being headless. They say that it is known as a shag-foal, as it has the appearance of a baby foal whose 'fuzz is giving way to its adult horsehair, hence the tatters'.[10] They believe these beasts could have been seen as petty demons during the Middle Ages and quote from the poet John Clare from 1821, who stated that it was a common myth in certain villages that the Devil sometimes appeared in the form of a 'shagg'd foal'.

Daniel Codd explains that nearer Scunthorpe, the creature is known as the Tatter Foal and lives in the marshlands around the area, tempting travellers and children into the bogs to be lost forever.

Apparently, human bones were found near the place where the Brigg sighting was reported and Westwood and Simpson quote Mabel Peacock, who believed it was possible that some of these creatures could have been the spirits of murder or suicide victims who had come back in the shape of an animal. Perhaps this is the reason these tortured souls wish to lead others astray, into the treacherous marshland.

Codd also mentions the legend of the sinister Dead Hand; this is the tale of a severed, bloody hand which grabs at passing travellers, pulling them into the swamps.

Polly Howat also mentions this legend when she retells the tale of poor Long Tom Pattison, whose foolhardy bravery led him to venture into the wetlands when no one else would go. He meant to show his superstitious friends that the bogs were not full of the evil things they believed lurked there, by volunteering to walk around them alone the following night.

Everyone tried to dissuade him, even his own mother, but these warnings only fuelled his desire to prove them wrong. He took his mother's lantern and ventured out into the marshes, followed at some safe distance by a group of young lads who wanted to watch what would happen to him. As Tom neared the bogs, a chill wind rose and blew out his lantern and then all the evil things that lived in the wetlands began to rise and close in around him. The group following could no longer see Tom, but could hear his shouts as he fought with the horrors surrounding him. They got closer and eventually could see Tom's face, looking pale as death, and they saw that he was being dragged further into the marshes by a 'hand without a body, known as the Dead Hand'.[11] The boys fled in terror and although search parties were dispatched at first light, Tom was not to be found.

In her despair, his poor mother began to lose her mind and one evening, over a month later, she was seen running from the marshes calling for help. She led the crowd, which had quickly gathered, back into the bogs and they discovered her son sitting there, with his feet in the water. He was aged beyond his years and was gibbering some nonsense and pointing at horrors only he could see. The other hand, the one that had been grasped by the Dead Hand, was missing and all that was left was a 'ragged stump'.

Tom never told what had happened to him but acted like a madman, always muttering to himself with wild eyes and every evening running out into the marshes again. The unfortunate boy and his mother were both found dead within the year; he was lying in his mother's lap, his expression one full of horror and torture, hers a look of contentment as she had at last found her boy. Both mother and son haunted those marshes ever after, along with the Dead Hand, contributing to the very stories Tom had hoped to dispel.

Adrian Gray says that even up until a few generations ago, the Lincolnshire Carrs were still very isolated places where strangers hardly ever ventured: '... they [the Carrs] were once dank, inhospitable and even rather frightening. They were home to all manner of unpleasant creatures, among which boggarts and bogles were the least pleasant of all.'[12]

Some believed prayers and secret chants would help protect them from these beasts and some even smeared blood around their doors. The word was that putting bread and salt out would please them and even help the success of their crop. The worst time was during the winter, when everything was dead and there was not much work to do. Bogles – naturally mischievous sprites – without any diversions, turned their attention to the people inhabiting the area. The locals obviously wished for the speedy arrival of spring to distract the bogles once more, and each day they would stand at their doors looking for the rising of the Green Mist which was said to signal the beginning of spring.

Legend tells of one particular family who were much troubled by the bogles one winter. The young daughter had become very sick and although doctors and priests had been called, the girl said the only thing that could save her was the arrival of the Green Mist. Every day, mother and daughter would wait at the door for the Green Mist to come and every day the ground was still hard with winter frost. The girl was convinced that if only she could live to see the cowslips bloom, she would die content with the arrival of summer. Her mother chided her for such words, saying she was tempting the wicked bogles to destroy her dreams with such suggestions.

The next day as she opened the curtains, the mother rejoiced at seeing the Green Mist. She carried her daughter out into the garden, and at the bottom by the gate the girl spied some small cowslips growing. Each day after that, the girl seemed to grow steadily stronger and when she was strong enough to go out, she would visit the cowslips every day and dance around them.

The healthy bloom that now filled her cheeks attracted the attention of a young man who passed by her gate every day. He saw how she loved the cowslips and one day, wishing to capture her heart, he picked some of the dainty flowers and offered them to her.

Her face, however, was a picture of horror. She turned quite white and, grasping the flowers from his hand, she flew inside and went straight to bed. Her mother found her very ill and called the doctor, but it seemed nothing could be done. The poor girl died within a few hours, still holding onto the flowers her sweetheart had offered her. Her mother was inconsolable; in her heart she knew her daughter's death was because of the unwitting challenge she had given the bogles.

Daniel Codd relates a legend told by folklorist Mrs Balfour from the late 1800s, about more mischief that the bogles of Lincolnshire caused in the Fens.[13] It is said that all manner of hideous creatures, including bogles, lived in the Fens and it was the task of the moon to chase away all the evils that lurked in the shadows, shining her light into the dark corners of the world. One night she decided to go and visit the sinister Fens and, wrapping herself in a black cloak, she made her way out into the dark, wet Carrs. She saw all the beasts and creatures she usually scared away; witches, boggarts, Will-o-the-Wisps and the souls of the dead rising from their watery graves. She wandered warily past but stepped on a loose stone and nearly fell in the marsh. She reached out to grasp a nearby tree to steady herself, but as soon as she touched it, the tree, Black Snag, stretched out its branches and wrapped her in its wooden embrace. She was terrified, unable to move and powerless to help as a poor lost traveller stumbled through the Fens. The stranger was lured off the dark path by the eerie, flickering lights of the Will-o-the-Wisp and disappeared into the dark. The moon struggled to free herself, knowing the traveller would surely meet a grisly end alone in the dark Fens, and as she struggled her cloak became loose and some of her tremendous light shone out. The light lit up the Fens as far as the eye could see and the moon saw the traveller realise his mistake and find the path again, moving safely on his way. The tree shifted and the cloak fell back over the moon, again hiding the light, but all the bogles and other evil creatures had seen it and became aware of her presence. When they realised she was trapped, they rejoiced and planned how to ensnare her forever. If her light never shone again they would be free to roam the marshes every night with nothing to fear. The creatures all gathered together and carried the moon to one of the deep pools. The dead pushed her down and then the others rolled a huge boulder over her to trap her under the water forever.

The people who lived round about watched apprehensively from their windows as there was no sight of the moon for the next few nights. They knew that without the light of the moon they were in great danger from the perils that lurked in the dark marshes, and it wasn't long before the bogles grew bolder and began to approach people's houses. The locals reverted to all the old ways of keeping them at bay; throwing out salt, wiping blood on the doors, placing a button on the window sill, but still no moon appeared.

One night some locals were gathered in the pub, all postulating on what could possibly have happened to the moon, when one man stepped forward and gave his opinion. He told them how he had been coming home across the Fens one night and had got lost in the dark. He explained how there had been a sudden bright light that had shown him the right path home and had saved his life. He said that he thought it had been the moon and that it was still there, trapped in the Fens. The men decided to go and try to free the moon. The traveller told them to look for the landmarks he remembered – a boulder shaped like a large coffin, a cross and a candle.

The men journeyed into the black Fens, jumping at every shadow and noise around them. Eventually they saw branches of a twisted, ancient bush that were shaped like a cross, upon which flickered a light, like a Will-o-the-Wisp, and they knew they were in the right area. They looked around and then they saw the tell-tale boulder half in a deep pool. The men gathered round the stone and said a silent prayer, and then they heaved the rock up and threw it on the bank. For a fraction of a second they found themselves gazing into the most beautiful face any of them had ever seen; then they were blinded by a dazzling light as the moon rose back up into the sky, reclaiming her place amongst the stars and forcing all the evil spirits back into the shadows. The men now had a safe journey home, in the full light of the grateful moon, and the bogles retreated to their holes.

Boston, once one of the most flourishing ports in England until the decline in trade around the time of Elizabeth I, due to the silting up of the River Witham, was known as a safe haven for travellers.

The famous tower, Boston Stump, is visible for miles around, views from the top reaching thirty-two miles and it was, at one time, used as a beacon, the lantern towering at a dizzy height of 272 feet, 'through which the Fenland wind blows an eerie note'.[14] The tower is said to have been used as a marker for

The Boston Stump, visible for miles around, especially since it is surrounded by such flat landscape.

travellers in the Fens and the Wash and it became very important again during the Second World War, as a landmark for pilots going back to base.

The Fens are one of the few places in Britain which, when the conditions are just right, create a secure, magical arena for ice skating in the long winter months. The weather has to coincide with the flooding of the low-lying marshes and farm land – if the ice comes too late, in February or March, often there is no water left to freeze and skating is impossible – but when the freeze comes just after the fields and meadows have flooded, it produces an ideal environment for skaters, safe in the knowledge that even if the ice does crack, the water is only an inch or so deep and so no real disaster can occur.

Skating on the Fens is an age-old tradition and, originally, the skaters used flattened animal bones strapped to their feet. Then improvements were made in the Victorian era and steel blades were introduced, adding new speed for the 'Fen runners'. The first people known to have started the trend were the farm workers who, with no farmland to work on in the frozen weather, started skating to keep warm! Then the inevitable competitions began and with no income from farming in such cold weather, racing for a loaf of bread or a slab of meat was plenty of motivation for the hungry souls. By the 1800s, Fen skating was a massive spectator sport and a National Skating Association was developed but, as previously mentioned, much depended on the right conditions. Coincidentally, at the time of writing this chapter those very conditions have presented themselves and many Fenland dwellers are dusting off the skates that have been packed away for years and are once again enjoying skating on the Fens.

The *Lincolnshire Life* magazine tells the story of a boggart who lived in the Fens. It explains that boggarts were wild creatures, half man half animal, who lived secretly in the small areas of wilderness left behind when the main areas of the Fen were drained. The magazine suggests they could have been descended from the 'slodgers'. Before the drainage in the nineteenth century, 'Fen slodgers' made their living catching fish and fowl on the wetlands of the Fens, for trading and survival. Legend implies some 'slodgers' never accepted the transformation of the Fens and stayed behind, hidden from people and scraping an existence. The *Lincolnshire Life* magazine explains that they were extraordinarily strong and were also rather sly and cunning.

This particular boggart lived in the Fenland near a farmer, who wanted to drain the area round-about and use it for growing crops. One day, after he had been out ploughing the area, the boggart confronted him and told him in no uncertain terms that the land belonged to him and that the farmer had to clear out: 'Most local men would have fled at first sight of the fearsome creature, with its ape-like stance, deep eye sockets and long, tangled hair; but the farmer, though apprehensive, stood his ground and engaged in argument.'[15]

The two, both believing the land was theirs, carried on arguing for some time until at last they reached an agreement. They decided that the farmer would till and sow the land but that they would share the end produce. The farmer would take what he grew in the soil and the boggart would have whatever grew above it.

They parted and didn't meet again until harvest time. The farmer, quite a cunning man himself, had grown potatoes and when he went to collect his crop he also took with him a large cudgel for protection, in case the boggart turned violent at this trickery. The boggart was visibly displeased when he saw the large mound of potatoes the farmer had, but after spying the cudgel in his hands, he allowed the farmer his crop. He insisted, however, that for the next crop things would be reversed; the boggart would have all that grew under the soil and the farmer would have whatever was on top. The farmer went home very happy, planning the crop of beans he would grow. Of course at the next harvest the boggart lost out again and so, realising he had been tricked, this time he insisted corn would be grown. At harvest time they would each start at an opposite corner of the field and cut at the same time until they met in the middle. The farmer had no choice but to agree, although he was uneasy about the deal. He knew that with the strength of ten men, the boggart would be much faster at cutting the corn and would take the farmer's share too. Just before harvest time the farmer crept out one night and laid some iron wires amongst the stalks in the boggart's half, then when the day came the boggart's blade was blunted in the first few strokes and the farmer ended up with more than his share of the crop. Luckily for the farmer, the boggart knew when he had met his match and left the area, never to be seen again.

Ethel Rudkin tells the story of another boggart who was often seen around Wildsworth, at Woofer Lane. The story goes that there was a party of poachers, around 1862, who were fishing along the Trent when they were frightened by the shrieking of otherworldly, mocking laughter. The men ran away, leaving their nets behind, all except one who was determined not to lose his equipment. That was until there was another blood-curdling shriek directly above him and then he was off with the others, net-less! The Woofer Boggard was a creature with a reputation and all the men had heard stories of it before but none had ever seen or heard it prior to that incident. Needless to say, none of them ever went back to poach there again.

The *Lincolnshire Life* magazine relates a sad tale situated around Monks Abbey in an area known as The Willows. A long time ago there was a beautiful lady who lived close to the banks of the swift-flowing River Witham. There was a legend that the river was magical, but it also had fast currents and deep pools within it. The lady was being wooed by a handsome knight with whom she was in love. He would ride out to meet her everyday and they would sit together on the banks of the river, below the weeping willows.

There was a small island out in a deeper pool of the river and there grew some of the prettiest flowers the lady had ever seen. They were the loveliest blue, like the summer sky, and so delicate that she longed to hold a bunch in her hands and smell their petals.

One spring day, when the birds were singing and the sun was shining down on the flowers, they shone even more brightly than before, the blue dazzling the beautiful lady, until she begged her sweetheart to fetch some for her. The noble knight loved his lady dearly and dutifully waded into the water to pick her the flowers. However, there was much deep, soft mud on the river bottom and his armour was very heavy in the water. He carried on regardless and made it to the island where he picked her the finest bunch of the blue flowers he could find. Then, holding them high above the water, he began to make his way back to her. He found the way back much harder, his feet, ankles and knees swallowed up in the mud. The current was tearing at his tiring legs and his armour was now so heavy that each step seemed like a thousand. He struggled to get back to her but was sinking rapidly and he realised he would not make it. Holding his head high and the flowers even higher, he called out to her, 'Forget me not, forget me not, forget me not!'[16] Then he was gone, sinking beneath the water, and the last thing she saw was her posy of blue flowers disappearing along with her lover. It is said that even now, on certain spring days, you can hear the sound of a lady crying and her brave knight calling to her.

Christopher Marlow tells of the story of a Louth girl, Fanny, known as Fan o' the Fens.[17] She was apparently renowned for her beauty and she lived in a cottage with her old widowed mother, near the moor. Her mother had been complaining of being harassed by a magpie that supposedly followed her everywhere, all through the day, repeating every word she said and generally tormenting her. Eventually, she was so perturbed that she asked the Wiseman of Louth to help her. He believed someone had placed a spell on her and called a meeting in her house, in front of the neighbours. He made everyone sit round in a circle and then said that the guilty person would be shown to them when the sleeping cat by the fire awoke and went to sit on their shoulder. Everyone watched with bated breath as, when the cat awoke, it circled round the group and then climbed up Fan's lap and then onto her shoulder, where it settled, purring contentedly. She was immediately branded a witch and the cat was labelled as her witch's familiar, sure evidence of her dark arts. Poor Fan o' the Fens was shunned by all the villagers and even her sweetheart, Simon Girsby, left her for another woman, Rose Hipkin. The lad, however, began to put on weight and everyone noticed that since leaving Fan, he was becoming fatter and fatter. He consulted a white wizard, who told him he was under the spell of a witch and that the witch would be revealed to him that very day, burning.

On the way home, Simon had to pass by Fan's house and as he did so, she ran out, covered in flames and screaming for help. She nearly died and was badly burnt but still protested her innocence. The spell seemed to have been lifted from Simon, however, and he was soon as slim as he had ever been.

People began to notice that Fan's temperament started to change and she began to play neighbours off against each other, causing trouble and seeming to hate the villagers as much as they hated her. One such neighbour was Thomas Friskney, who had to pass her house every day, but each time his horses refused to go past the cottage, until one day he was so fed up that he shouted a curse on all witches. Fan was seen to overhear him and some time later, Thomas was taken ill with great pain in his chest. It was discovered

The ruins of Monks Abbey, Lincoln. Found along Monks Road, the abbey once stood beside a leafy lane in open fields, above the deep River Witham. Now the ruins are situated within a housing estate, having being swallowed up by the city.

he had a live snake inside him and the villagers had to use an old method of tempting the snake out with a bowl of fresh milk, as that is the only way to lure a snake out, if you should ever accidentally swallow one, tail first!

It was rumoured that Fan o' the Fens would regularly fly out on a stick to meet the Devil in the dark marshes when there was a full moon and the people decided to try and catch her in the act. The only drawback was that if one were to see this Devil worshipping on the night of a full moon, it was certain the watcher would die within the year – only a wiseman was exempt from the rule. So, the local wiseman was appointed the task of watching Fan's house and settled himself in the bushes opposite on the night in question. After a while, he heard voices and chanting coming from an upstairs room, then a window opened and he watched Fan fly out on a broom, followed by numerous other witches. He entered the house and searched her room, finding evidence of Devil worship, and then went back to hide in the bushes. When Fan and the others arrived back at dawn, the wiseman knocked loudly on her door. He pushed past her when she opened it and stormed to her room to catch the others, but the room was empty and all signs of Devil worship had disappeared. Only Fan was left, so he caught her and took her to the local constable. The girl was put on trial, where

The River Lud, which runs through Louth.

many gave evidence against her, including the wiseman and Simon Girsby, but it was deemed that there was not sufficient proof to condemn her. She was freed, but some of the villagers and the wiseman were so outraged that they forced their way into her house and took the poor girl to the local pond. There they gave her the ultimatum of either confessing to being a witch, or being plunged into the river. Of course, the girl confessed and said all the allegations against her were true but the villagers were in such a frenzy now that they submerged Fan into the river anyway and nearly drowned her. Then they beat her with sticks and drove her out of the village with warnings never to return. The locals celebrated the expulsion of the witch and Fan o' the Fens was never seen in those parts again.

It was not just the Fens and Marshes that were the source of such treacherous tales. The extensive Lincolnshire coast had its fair share of stories too. Fishing was at one point a huge industry in Lincolnshire. Grimsby was once the largest fish dock in the country and in 1923 it boasted that eight complete train loads of fish were dispatched every day. Some say it was arguably the largest fishing port in the world.

Being a fisherman was a hard life and there are numerous tragic stories concerning fishermen who have been lost at sea, whole ships never returning and families and widows left behind to mourn the drowned crew.

A fisherman is a man with the sky
in his eyes and saltwater in his veins.
A man who knows that every time
he leaves his home harbour, he might
never see it again.

In tiny vessels they defy,
the perils of the deep,
and scan the water's dreary wastes,
With eyes that never sleep.[18]

One story, however, related in 'Fish 'n' Ships', tells of Fred Lambert's close shaves with death at the hands of the monstrous sea. He was only a young lad of sixteen when he began the life of a fisherman. He says it was Christmas morning and their ship was out in a cold North Sea storm and he could see some huge waves coming at him. He didn't have much time to react and the next thing he knew, the sea had washed him over the side of the ship. Luckily, as he says often happens, the sea washed him back again, whereby the skipper was able to grab him and push him to safety before he went overboard again. He had the courage to go to sea again and, amazingly, the same thing happened to him twice more in the span of his fishing career, again in rough seas and the same skipper hauled him to safety! His wife, Christine told her reaction: 'Horrified. I was horrified. Though he didn't tell me for ages. But you get to the stage where if they go over three times they say the sea doesn't want them…That helps to keep me sane.'

There are numerous superstitions connected with the fishing life. Christine Lambert was told never to do any washing the day her husband set sail because if she did, it was like washing him away. Another belief was that one should always give silver to a baby. If the baby gripped the coin it meant the fisherman would have a good trip. Dutchy Holland took his three-year-old daughter down to the docks while he went to collect his pay. When they were ready to leave, his daughter began to cry and said she couldn't walk. Thinking she wanted to be carried, Dutchy went to pick her up and found that he could hardly lift the child; her pockets were so full of coins that the fishermen round about had given her.

Fishermen's wives believed that it was all right to go and meet their husbands when they came into dock, but it was unlucky to see them off. It was also unlucky for them to wear green. *Deep Sea Voices* tells of one wife who spent a long time knitting her husband a beautiful green sweater, which he downright refused to take with him for fear of bad luck. Many fishermen's wives believed it was bad luck to knit at all when their husbands were at sea, as it was believed that in doing so they would snag his net. His catch would then be lost and their livelihood badly affected.

The *Lincolnshire Life* magazine tells us that there were quite a few taboo words within the fishing community, which fishermen should not speak whilst they were out at sea.[19] Rats were referred to as long tails, rabbits were bob tails and pigs were curly tails. The men also believed it was unlucky to whistle whilst at sea, as it would whistle up a dangerous wind. It was fine to whistle on dry land, or to use the word pig, and this is one theory as to why there are so many pubs named the 'Pig and Whistle' along the coast.

Folklorists Gutch and Peacock talk of a number of superstitions concerning water. In the neighbourhood of Kirton-in-Lindsey, it was believed that no washing ought to be done on Ascension Day, since, if clothes are hung out to dry on Holy Thursday, some member of the family concerned would die. They also state that whenever water is drawn from a well, a little should be thrown back into it. There are many instances throughout Lincolnshire of wells that have healing properties. In Lower Burnham, on the festival of the Ascension, the water in the well was supposed to cure all sorts of deformities and diseases, especially in children. A spring at Burnham was also thought to be able to cure sterility in married women. Another spring at Lincoln was said to cure bad legs and many physical ailments. There are numerous wells that are believed to have the beneficial properties of being able to heal the eyes. A well near Stamford apparently had powers to restore sight to the blind; one near Caistor was supposed to heal diseased eyes. Bathing in the waters of a now-vanished spring at Bottesford healed blindness and other physical complaints, and another at Barnetby-le-Wold healed the diseased eyes of children. My favourite belief is that drinking from the wells at Kirton had the quality of '... giving those who drink of it an irresistible desire to live in its neighbourhood.'[20]

Fishermen might not agree – after inhaling lung fulls of the stuff out in stormy waters – but the drinking of seawater was once recommended for medicinal purposes. Dubbed 'Neptune's Ale', it was first suggested in the 1600s and still considered beneficial during the late 1700s. Reverend John Wesley himself vowed it was invaluable to help cure swollen glands and recommended drinking seawater every day for a week to help treat shingles. I am not sure how many would want to try it now...

It was not just the treacherous conditions of the storms and bad weather at sea that fishermen feared. People have been drowned in the mud banks and dangerously soft sand around Mablethorpe, and the stealthy speed of the incoming tide at the Wash has claimed its share of victims too.

> The Wash mud is clammy and cold
> Here King John lost his riches of old –
> This may happen again
> It's increasingly plain,
> Only this time it's your and my gold.[21]

The legend of King John losing his treasure in the sudden turn of the waters in the Wash is well known. He supposedly misjudged the time of the high tide and had to flee the clutches of the quicksand and treacherous undercurrents, abandoning his gold to the muddy depths. Charles Dickens refers to this

The Wash, where King John is said to have lost his treasure.

unfortunate incident in his *A Child's History of England*: 'Looking back from the shore when he was safe, he saw the roaring water sweep down in a torrent, overturn the wagons, horses, and men, that carried his treasure, and engulf them in a raging whirlpool from which nothing could be delivered.'

However, beware when searching for the lost treasure, as there is also a story about a beast that dwelt in the deeps off the coast of Mablethorpe. Some kind of sea creature had been spotted off the Brigg at Filey and many thought it then made its way to the Lincolnshire coast. Its appearance has been reported on occasion for numerous years and its description is slightly akin to that of the Loch Ness Monster. Locals tell of a 'thing' with a humped back and swift movement through the water.

Daniel Codd reports another monster that was seen in 1743 in the Fossdyke Wash. Some fishermen apparently caught it, stating that it was 8 feet long, with webbed feet. Ethel Rudkin apparently also mentioned the story of a beast spotted in 1936 in the River Trent. It had large eyes, long shaggy hair and walrus-like tusks!

Like many other areas of the country, smuggling was, of course, rife for a time along the Lincolnshire coast, as was ship-wrecking. Polly Howat retells the story of the *Mary Rose*, which set sail from Scotland in 1629, bound for Plymouth.[22] When the ship was near the Lincolnshire coast the weather turned stormy. Poor visibility developed, coupled with fierce winds and lashing rain, which was unfortunate for the crew, but just the conditions that some of the inhabitants of Burgh-le-Marsh were waiting for. They had a beacon upon Marsh Hill, which they often lit to lure ships into danger, in order to loot

The Burgh-le-Marsh beacon, situated next to the church, on a small hill within a field next to the main road.

them. However, they decided that on this night, the light would be construed as a warning, so it was better to leave the ship alone in the dark to face the inevitable disaster which would befall it in such a storm.

The Sexton Guymer, however, felt moved to help the poor wretches and so he took himself off to St Peter's and locked himself in the belfry. The old man began to ring the great bell, Grandsire Bob, hoping the ship's crew would hear it and be warned away from the coast. The villagers certainly heard it and ran to the church to stop the old man. They were furious but, hard as they tried, they were unable to break into the church. Guymer pulled and pulled on the bell and managed to keep ringing Grandsire Bob for a whole hour. The warning was heeded by the crew of the *Mary Rose* and they managed to steer away from the danger. When the villagers finally broke the church door down they found poor Guymer dead, still grasping onto the bell rope as if continuing his mission in death. Legend states that the captain returned to the village the following year to express his thanks for saving his life. When he learnt the truth, he apparently bought an acre of land in Orby Field, which he named Bell String Acre, and with the money he earned in rent he bought a new silken rope for Grandsire Bob.

As well as ship wreckers and actual monsters, there have been some terrible monster storms which have devastated the coastline along Lincolnshire. One of the worst was the great storm of January 1953, in Mablethorpe, which claimed forty-one lives within just a few short hours. *The Book of the Lincolnshire Seaside* mentions the sad tale of four elderly people who were amongst the forty-one drowned. Annie Millward had made a prior arrangement with her neighbours that they could ring the bell connected between their houses if they ever needed help. On that fateful day, however, Annie herself was marooned and could only listen in horror as the bell's insistent ringing grew quiet.

The sea was not the only water to be feared, as the tragedy of the Louth flood shows. On a rainy day, 29 May 1920, the usually peaceful River Lud broke its banks and caused a catastrophic flood in the town. Meteorologists suggested the cause was a 'cloud burst' some six miles away, which had then swept down the valley gathering such momentum that within half an hour of the Lud breaching its banks, it had risen to an unbelievable 15 feet above its usual level. Houses were swept away, bridges toppled, people were trapped and twenty-three died in the flood that day, including children. In one tragic incident a mother was trapped with her four young children. She apparently lifted three of them onto the kitchen dresser then climbed up herself with her baby in her arms. As the water level rose, she hung on to a hook in the ceiling and the three young ones clung onto her dress, until one by one they could no longer hold on and they were swept out of her grasp, only to drown before her very eyes. The mother and baby were rescued sometime later. There is a memorial stone in the town cemetery to all those who lost their lives, reading, 'Let not the waterflood overwhelm me, neither let the deep swallow me up.'

The memorial stone to commemorate those who lost their lives during the Great Flood of Louth, 1920.

There was a time when the Fens were often flooded and after a few days the area looked as it had before it was drained. It happened so often that there were flood laws that everyone adhered to, which Katherine Briggs relates in Barrett's *Tales of the Fens*. The laws stated that anything found floating in the flood waters had to be taken to Stack's Hill at Southery, where the owners would be able to find it. If it had not been claimed after a certain time then those who had found it could claim it for their own. Also, if anyone was found robbing a house the penalty was quite severe; their boat would be smashed to pieces and the robbers left in the flooded house for a week, starving. They could try and swim away but, if not, a boat would come by in a week to pick them up, if they were still alive: 'This law was kept so well that a man could leave his watch on the mantelshelf and know it would still be there when he went back for it.'[23]

It was also stated that no man should go out alone in a boat and this was a rule created after an unpleasant incident had occurred. A man had been flooded out and rowed back to his house, but when he arrived he disturbed two gypsies robbing his home. His boat was found the next day and when a search for him was organised, he was found sitting in his bedroom with an axe in his skull.

The tale goes, however, that the gypsies rammed a gatepost in their haste to flee the scene of the crime and ripped the bottom from their boat. They could not swim and so clung onto the gatepost shouting for help. The locals, finding the poor dead man, decided to teach the gypsies a lesson and tied his dead body on the gatepost with them for a day and a night!

Water, in whatever guise, is the stuff of life and Lincolnshire certainly has its fair share of both. The multitude of stories and legends connected to the Fens, marshes, rivers and the sea are colourful and varied and these tales, along with the beauty of the area, make it a wonderful place to visit.

# 3

# BLACK DOGS AND STRANGE ENCOUNTERS

The Black Dog is a frequently reported apparition in British folklore; an unusually large, jet black, dog-like beast, often with glowing eyes, appearing in solitary places. Every county has its stories of this sinister phenomenon, each with a differing name; in Lincolnshire they are called either Black Shuck or Hairy Jack.

It is said that Sir Arthur Conan Doyle took inspiration from tales of the Yeth Hounds, the beasts that are said to roam Dartmoor, when he wrote *The Hound of the Baskervilles*. Other famous authors have absorbed some of this folklore into their writings, such as Charlotte Brontë in *Jane Eyre*, showing the sightings and tales were well enough known to be included in popular writing.

> The din was on the causeway: a horse was coming…In those days I was young, and all sorts of fancies bright and dark tenanted my mind…I remembered certain of Bessie's tales, wherein figured a North-of-England spirit, called a 'Gytrash'; which, in the form of a horse, mule, or large dog, haunted solitary ways, and sometimes came upon belated travellers, as this horse was now coming upon me…I heard a rush under the hedge, and [there] glided a great dog…It was exactly one mask of Bessie's Gytrash – a lion-like creature with long hair and a huge head.[1]

Theo Brown identifies three separate types of Black Dogs but she does admit to there being some overlap:

> A. That which is generally known locally as the Barguest, Shuck, Black Shag, Trash, Skriker, Padfoot and other names. These are not the names of individuals but of an impersonal creature which is distributed over certain areas…This type, which we may call the Barguest type, changes its shape, a thing that no true Black Dog ever does.

The only pond left visible along the road from Leverton to Wrangle.

> B. That which is nearly always known as the Black Dog, is always black, and is always a dog and nothing else…It is always associated with a definite place or 'beat' on a road. It is always an individual. Sometimes it is associated with a person or a family…Another personal association is that with witches.
>
> C. A third variety of Black Dog, which is rare, is that which appears in a certain locality in conjunction with a calendar cycle.[2]

As well as the Barguest and other names she mentions above, the Black Dog is also known as the Gurt Dog, Dando Dogs, Wish Hounds, Moddey Dhoo, Pooka and Hooter, just to name a few. Some sources suggest that the creature known as the Shagfoal in Lincolnshire is another manifestation of the Black Dog.

No one seems very sure as to why they materialise; some suggest they are portents of death, others that they appear in order to carry dead souls away, but some believe they are benevolent creatures sent to protect people, especially women on their own, in lonely places.

There was apparently a sighting by a woman at Blyborough, who was followed by a Black Dog along the road by the village pond. She hit out at the creature with her umbrella, but the object passed straight through it. We do not know what happened to the dog but can assume the lady made it home safely, as her story survives.[3]

The church at Algarkirk, although no Black Dog was to be seen here this day.

Briggs adds that with the three types of dog Brown mentions, there can also be added demon dogs, ghosts of dogs and even ghosts of humans taking dog form.[4] She believes there are equal numbers of stories of the Black Dog being benevolent as there are of it being malevolent – a guardian or a devilish creature.

There were so many sightings of the Black Dog in Lincolnshire that folklorist Ethel Rudkin dedicated an entire book to the field. Writing in the 1930s, she claimed to have seen the Black Dog herself in the county, and talked to many others who had shared her experience. According to Rudkin, more often than not the Lincolnshire Black Dog is benevolent.

She talks of a man who used to cycle home from Leverton to Wrangle and often saw the Black Dog appear near a long, deep pond. It would run so far along the road then turn down an adjacent lane each time it appeared.

One Mrs B was reported to have seen the Black Dog at Algarkirk, where she lived, near the trees that grew near to the church. 'It is tall and thin, with a long neck and pointed nose. It leaps into the road and runs before the spectator, leaping back over another gate farther on. It always comes and goes on one's left.'[5]

Another regular sighting was in and around Bourne Wood. Many people said they saw the dog and that it seemed quite friendly but would never allow anyone to stroke it, always leaving them at the same place every time, a gate in the corner of the wood.

The little bridge that crosses the stream near Manton, where the Black Dog was reportedly seen.

Rudkin says the road up to Moortown Hall was also haunted by the dog. It apparently appeared in the exact same spot in the hedge every time and some people claimed they felt it brushing past their legs.

One of the indoor sightings of the Black Dog was within a house in Brigg. It was converted into a shop later on, but during the time of the Reformation, a Catholic family was said to live there, with a private chapel hidden away in the roof. The house was allegedly haunted, with strange noises being heard and doors opening and closing for no apparent reason. The spectre of a large Black Dog with huge, glowing eyes was often reported; and the rumour was that it was the spirit of a woman who had been murdered in the house, appearing in the form of this dog. It was said to never leave the house, adopting guardianship of the old altar.

An additional sighting was along a green lane at Manton, where the Black Dog was seen near the bridge that crosses the stream.

Also at Bransby, where the River Till flows, the Black Dog has supposedly been spotted walking down Bonnewells Lane. This is apparently a very haunted place. Rudkin mentioned the ghosts of a lady in a rustling silk dress, a sow with her litter and even Oliver Cromwell. She reproduced a poem of the lane, written by Muriel M. Andrew, entitled 'The Legend of the Ghost in Bonny Wells Lane':

'E set off down owd Bonny Wells lane
At just a fairish paace,
When summat big an' grey 'e seed,
He tonned 'im round in 'aaste.

It sure unnerved 'im, that it did,
To be theer by 'issen,
Until 'e thote about the Dog,
He warn't so freentened then.

He couldn't see the big Black Dog,
What should be i' the Laane,
Protectin' all good foalks, they say,
(The bad 'uns look in vain).[6]

The poem implies that the Black Dog in this lane was seen as something of a guardian, especially as the lane was haunted by other spectres, and the dog helped protect the good people. The fact that it was mentioned in the poem shows the legend was a long-standing local belief. The poor fellow in this particular tale, after running home for help and coming back with some other men, was shown to be a fool, as it transpired that the large grey creature he saw was none other than a braying donkey.

The reputedly haunted Bonnewells Lane, Bransby.

Daniel Codd relates a story of a Black Dog haunting a small cottage in Gainsborough in 1823.[7] This creature seemed to be more on the malevolent side than Rudkin's apparitions, delivering sinister tappings at the window, door and bedposts. It also exhibited poltergeist behaviour, often directed towards a young girl in the house and, as far as Codd is concerned, the creature was never banished.

On his webpage, Dr Simon Sherwood describes an experience of the Black Dog he had as a child, living in Spalding in the 1970s.[8] He recalls how he was asleep in bed, when he was suddenly woken by the patter of feet. When he opened his eyes he saw a huge dog, with horns, sprinting along the hall towards his bedroom. The dog had massive, bright yellow eyes and when it reached the door to the bedroom it disappeared. The boy's scream attracted his mother's attention and she persuaded him it had merely been the reflection of car headlights. It was only later, as an adult, whilst reading the newspaper that he came across a story of a poltergeist haunting in a council house. Apparently a number of objects had been thrown at the baby in the house, and the father also said he had seen a large, dark dog run at him, then disappear. This particular story would seem in accordance with Codd's poltergeist Black Dog – more on the evil side than Rudkin's reported experiences.

Sean McNeaney describes a malevolent Black Dog, witnessed by a farm worker somewhere on the outskirts of Hemswell.[9] He is said to have inadvertently dug up the bones of some large animal. He presumed it to be a donkey or calf, but on closer inspection he saw it possessed rather ferocious-looking canine teeth. He placed the skull in a sack and decided to take it along to his local pub to show his friends. It was a cold, dark winter's night and the journey was along narrow isolated lanes. When he was but halfway, he was overcome with a feeling of dread and began to glance over his shoulder at regular intervals, although he saw nothing untoward. Shortly, however, he heard the sound of heavy, lumbering padded feet and the panting of some huge creature fast approaching. This time when he looked behind, his eyes fell on a massive Black Dog, running at him with bared teeth and burning red eyes. The horrified man began to run but the creature quickened its pace and was soon upon him. He could feel its breath on the back of his neck, and he only had the sack of bones to protect him. With this in mind he suddenly turned and slammed the sack into the head of the beast and the bag tore, spilling the bones all around the two figures. As the bones crashed to the ground, splintering into fragments, the hound gave a horrific howl and then vanished right before his eyes. The poor man's friends laughed at his tale, at first, but soon began to believe him, when his deathly-pale expression did not change, and ever after the farm worker was terrified of all dogs.

The Black Dog is not the only supernatural canine creature to inhabit Lincolnshire. Strangely enough, there are also reports of werewolf sightings, which some find harder to believe than the Black Dog apparitions.

Daniel Codd tells the tale of a certain wolf man who used to inhabit Read's Island about 200 years ago. There was a travelling vagabond, who had built himself a small shelter on the island and earned his living rowing people across the waters in his small boat. During his stay on the island, however, it is said that there were frequent mysterious disappearances and eventually one passenger tipped off the authorities and the drifter was taken before the courts and accused of cannibalism. More evidence presented itself when the island was searched and hundreds of human bones were found scattered around his abode. Quite why there was so much traffic to this small island is never explained. The most disturbing part of the story tells that, during the trial, the traveller 'collapsed vomiting on to all fours, howling like an animal. His appearance began to take on the form of a monstrous wolf and there was an immense struggle to subdue him.'[10] No other information is given, except that he was hauled off to the countryside and then hanged. No one knows who he was or where he came from, least of all why he metamorphosed into a wolf.

There is another story, based in the neighbourhood of Gedney Dyke, concerning a witch by the name of Old Mother Nightshade. On account of her strange habits and the noises she made, she was feared by all those who lived nearby except one young lad, John Culpepper. The poor lad was something of a simpleton and found himself in the witch's lair one day, seeking advice on matters of the heart, after being spurned by the village beauty, Rose Taylor.

The old witch gave the boy a box of sweetmeats which he was to offer to the lady in question, then after three days he was to return to her. The lad obeyed these instructions and on the night of the full moon he found himself again in the

Read's Island, a small piece of land not far from the bank, in the River Humber. The Humber Bridge can be seen from its shores.

presence of the witch. 'Close your eyes until I tell you to open them,' the witch commanded. John did as he was bidden and eventually a strange, distorted voice told him to open them. The young man was aghast when he opened his eyes to see before him a gigantic wolf-like creature with long, shaggy hair looming over him. The poor lad, now tied to the chair, realised too late that he had been tricked, and the wolf-woman bore down on him and ripped him to shreds. The villagers all cowed behind their locked doors that night, hearing the screams and ungodly howls which filled the air, and in the morning the witch was gone and John's ragged remains were all that was left. Some huge, bloodied paw prints led off into the Fens, too big to belong to a dog, and the villagers realised at last what the witch had been. The cottage was burnt to the ground, but still the wolf's howl can sometimes be heard echoing across the Fens on the night of a full moon.

It is said that in those times, perhaps around the eighteenth century, it was believed that witches possessed the knowledge to mix certain ingredients into an ointment which, when rubbed on the skin, transformed them into a wolf-like creature. Another tale reinforces this idea; that of an old wizard who lived in Northorpe, near Bourne. He is reputed to have been seen turning into one of these wolf-like creatures and attacking his neighbour's cattle. At least it wasn't his neighbour!

Britain has relatively few werewolf stories, compared with some other countries in the world, but this could be due to the fact that wolves have been extinct here for such a long time and folklore concerning them has died out. There are only a few remaining stories, and luckily Lincolnshire is one area that still has some of these tales.

The area where the werewolf bones were supposedly dug up, aptly named Dogdyke.

Codd narrates a legend from the 1800s of a student who discovered the bones of a human skeleton with a wolf's head in the peatland near Dogdyke. He was so excited with his unusual find that he took the bones home in order to study them more closely. That night, however, he was woken by a tapping at the window. When he looked outside into the night he saw 'a moving, black shape; peering closer the form defined itself as a human being with a wolf's head, which was looking at him through the glass and snarling viciously. The creature drew back its clawed arm to smash the glass...'[11]

Of course, the young man fled, terrified, into the adjacent room where he could barricade himself in; he sat 'frozen with fear' for the rest of the night, listening to the prowling and padding sounds of the wolf creature in his house. In the morning, after he was sure the sounds had ceased, he ventured into the rest of the house, which had been turned upside down. The terrified lad immediately took the bones back to where he had found them and buried them deep in the peat. He never saw the beast again.

Christopher Marlowe mentions a few of these werewolf stories and adds another about an artist who was visiting the Fens around Crowland on a break from her home in London.[12] She was staying with a family and was on the way home to their farm one evening when she came across a local widow wandering in the lane. The lady seemed to be acting rather oddly and lagged behind the artist. As she looked back, the widow suddenly seemed to drop to her knees in the lane and then, before her very eyes, she watched her transform into a horrifying wolf creature. The werewolf came at the artist and she had the presence of mind to shine her pocket torch into the creature's eyes. It vanished immediately. When she arrived back at the farmhouse she found the widow there, and the family said she had been in their presence all the time but had at one point fallen to the floor complaining she had been blinded by lightning. In this instance, Marlowe proposes that she had telepathically projected herself to attack the artist, in the form of a wolf. This theory fits the idea that witches could transform themselves into wolf creatures – but she went even one step further, by projecting that form in one place while simultaneously being present as a human elsewhere.

One wonders at the popular tales depicted in books and films in today's world, of werewolves, vampires, zombies and the like. There is such a common theme amongst these stories, based on folk tales from all around the world, that there must be a grain of truth to them, no matter how far removed from the creatures on the big screen today.

Codd talks of a fear of zombie-like creatures being prevalent in Lincolnshire in the 1800s.[13] Apparently, some workmen dug up a skeleton of a man at Yaddlethorpe Hill, Bottesford. This man had been buried with a stake driven through his chest, which was apparently common practice with suicides. The recovered body would have a stake driven through the heart and then the corpse would be buried in quicklime at some crossroads, for faster disintegration, for fear it would rise again.

Folklorists Gutch and Peacock relate a similar tale, told to them by the rector of Wispington, about a dead fellow who was placed in his coffin overnight, but the next morning the body had disappeared and in its place was a pile of stones.[14]

They go on to say that it was the custom in Lincolnshire to always tie together the feet of the dead when the body was placed in the coffin, otherwise there was the fear that they could return or that some other spirit may take over the body. They use the example of Old Will Richardson, of Croft, whose feet were not tied when he died. Two weeks later, a visitor went round to the widow's house and was greeted by the daughter, who explained her mother was in rather a state. She realised she had forgotten to tie her late husband's feet together in his coffin and that he had come back and seated himself in the corner. They were too terrified to move him. On inspection, the visitor saw a huge toad sitting beneath the old man's chair and the belief was that the old man had come back in this form – something which could have been avoided if his feet had been tied.

Westwood and Simpson tell the tale of another frightening creature that visited an old gentleman in his bedroom at night, in South Ferriby.[15] They say that the old man could never have a good night's rest, as the curtains around his bed would draw themselves back and forth and then twist around his neck, as if to strangle him. One night other objects around the house began to move and make a terrible racket and so the man had to admit to his daughter what had been happening. He informed her that the apparition had told him he must go out that very night and meet the fiend on the hill behind the church, alone. He was too frightened to go and so ignored the order, but as he was ascending the stairs to bed that night something grabbed him on the way and tried to strangle him there and then. He agreed he would go to the hill and so the next night he set out alone, as requested, and when he returned he was visibly shaken. When his daughter questioned him about what had happened, he refused to discuss it and told her never to ask him again, but promised that it was finished and the thing would bother them no more. He was true to his word, but to what cost we shall never know.

Another strange beast that has gained notoriety in Lincolnshire is Yallery Brown. This particular story is thought to have occurred at Kirton-in-Lindsey and concerns a fellow named Tom Tiver. The tale tells that Tom was taking a stroll one summer's evening when he heard the cries of a baby. Thinking there was an abandoned or lost child in the long grass of the field he began to search anxiously. As he neared the sounds, they changed to a small voice calling out, complaining about being trapped under a heavy stone. He continued on and came to a large stone slab in the grass and realised the voice was coming from underneath it. Even though he had heard stories of strange creatures that came out especially at night, his heart was full of pity and Tom heaved over the great stone and watched a tiny little figure crawl out. Ragged clothes fell around his yellowy-brown skin and a scowling face peered out from the folds. The creature was not particularly friendly, but did say he would be Tom's friend for ever, since he had saved him. He also said he would grant Tom one wish for his good deed and after some thought, Tom said he would like a helping hand at his work. He thanked the tiny thing for the wish and at this the creature flew into a terrible rage. 'Never thank me!' he cried. When he had calmed down, he advised Tom to call for him if he ever needed any help, telling him his name was Yallery Brown. He then disappeared and the perplexed lad set off for home.

When he arrived at work the next day, he found all his tasks had been done for him already and so he just put his feet up and relaxed all day. This happened again the next day and the one after that and so on, until the other farm labourers began to get annoyed at his laziness and the fact that his jobs were being done for him. There were even rumours that little people had been seen at night doing his work, and not only that but their work was being undone! Where his buckets were filled, theirs were tipped over; while his tools were sharpened, theirs became blunt.

Seeing the discontent, Tom tried to look willing but whenever he tried to do any work he was not allowed – the broom would fly out of his hold and seemingly brush the floor itself or the plough would move away from his grasp. In the end the lad was fired from his job.

So angry was he that he called out for Yallery Brown to show himself, but when the creature did arrive he was so surprised that he politely asked for the help to cease and thanked him again for what he had done. A sinister look crossed the creature's face and he told the boy that the help would certainly stop, but as he had said thank you again he was now stuck with the Yallery Brown dogging him through all his life! He vanished, singing an ominous song:

Wok 's tha will,
Tha'll niver do well,
Wok 's tha mowt,
Tha'll niver gain owt,
For harm an' mischance an' Yallery Bro-wun
Tha's let oot theesen from unner th' sto-wun.

Poor Tom only met with misfortune after this; he lost every job he managed to get, his marriage broke down and his children died. His own attempt at farming failed, all his crops dying, and through each disaster Tom heard the cruel laugh of Yallery Brown echoing behind him.

The *Lincolnshire Life* magazine narrates a story with another cunning figure who tried to ensnare a respectable maiden.[16] The man in question was called Mr Fox and he was trying to court the young girl, much to her parents' dismay, as he had a reputation for being a bit of a rogue.

On one particular day, the young lass was sent out to do an errand by her father but, before she set off, a message arrived telling her to meet Mr Fox at the crossroads in Paddy Lane on her way home later. She knew of his reputation and realised it was rather a remote place to meet him, but she was flattered by his attention and also curious to know what he wanted. After her errand, she made her way to Paddy Lane but found that Mr Fox wasn't there. She was feeling somewhat nervous and so decided to hide from view and wait for him to arrive, so she found a tall tree and climbed up. After a while she saw Mr Fox approaching and was just about to call out to him, when she saw him bring out a spade he had hidden behind a bush. She waited to see what he was going to do with it and was amazed to see him digging what seemed to be a grave. She could only assume the grave was meant for her, so she kept very quiet and hid from him until he decided to leave. He waited a long time for the girl to show up, but when it got dark he lost his patience and stormed away in a rage. She then slipped down from the tree and ran home, telling her parents all that she had seen when she arrived. They made sure the story was passed around the area quickly and Mr Fox disappeared, no one around there ever seeing him again. Who he was or why he wanted to murder the girl are questions that remain unanswered.

It is not just creatures and strange beasts that behave in a reprehensible manner. There is a story, retold by Westwood, about the old man of Winterton.[17] Mr Lacy was a very rich man with three sons and when he got older, he decided he would split his fortune between the three whilst still living, on the condition that they should each keep him for a week, in turn, until his death. The sons agreed, pleased to have his money early, but after a while they each became weary of having him with them and started to treat him badly. They were mean to him, leaving him neglected, cold and hungry and treating him no better than a dog.

The old man was getting very upset and fed up with being treated like this and so went to visit a good friend of his, who was also an attorney. His friend told him there was nothing to be done legally to enforce better behaviour. He did, however, suggest an idea to his old friend:

> As you have always been good to me over the years I will lend you a strong box with £1,000 inside. Keep the box locked but at each of your sons' houses make a show of bringing out the box and counting the money inside. Make sure you lock the box again afterwards each time, but talk about it to keep reminding them of its existence. Their greed will soon have them treating you better, especially if you add that the son who treats you the best in the time you have left will receive the greater share upon your death.

Mr Lacy liked the idea very much and received the box a few days later. He did just as his attorney friend had suggested and when his sons saw there was more money to be had from their father, they began to change their behaviour towards him. He was given the best room at each house, the nicest food, fine wine and generally treated like a king. After a month the old man went back to his attorney friend and told him of the changes. He thanked him profusely and returned the box of money to him, although he told his sons that he had hidden the money again until the day he needed it.

The sons continued to treat their father with this renewed respect for the rest of his life, all because of the promise of more money. Just before he died he told them there was no money and reprimanded them for their bad behaviour in the past, but forgave them on his death bed, even though they had acted like beasts to their own kin.

There is also a rather well-known story about Jesus Christ visiting Lincolnshire, and having a run-in with a selfish farmer who owned Fonaby Top farm. The story, as retold by Polly Howat,[18] tells that Jesus was riding his ass through the fields near this farm, when he saw the farmer sowing some corn. He slowed down his hungry animal and enquired if the farmer could spare some of the corn for the ass. The farmer, not realising who the stranger was, lied and said that he had no corn. When Jesus asked what was in the sacks in the corner of the field, the farmer insisted they were full of stones. 'Then stone be it,' Jesus is said to have replied, and the sacks immediately turned to stone. Jesus went on his way but the farmer could not carry on with sowing, as he had no more corn!

The large sack stones also began to get in the way when he was ploughing later in the year and eventually he decided to move them. It was a large undertaking and took twenty-two horses in all to shift the stones from Fonaby Top down to the farmyard at Fonaby Bottom. Only then the farmer began to experience really bad luck; his crops started to fail and his cattle became ill and died, until eventually he believed the sack stones were to blame and had them taken back up to Fonaby Top. This time it only took one horse to drag them up the steep hill.

Word soon spread that the stones had some mystical properties and when it was known Jesus had passed that way, the whole story was revealed and many people came to see them. With time, the stones fell into three pieces so they are not very recognisable today, and though lying on private land they can still be seen.

Whilst visiting the area, I enquired at the farm, Fonaby Top, as to whether the stones were still visible. I was met by Mrs Rose Cole, who was extremely welcoming and invited me in for tea and homemade cakes. She kindly showed me the remains of the stones and told me that superstition around them was still prevalent today. They were half hidden in the undergrowth and she explained they had built the field boundary hedges along that section to cover the stones, so they would not be disturbed. Touching them was still seen as rather unwise. Mrs Cole even went on to tell me how her husband, Mason, had once accidentally nudged the stones with his combine harvester and broken his arm in the process!

What exactly Jesus was doing in Lincolnshire remains a mystery, although some versions of the story assert that the stranger was St Paul, not Christ. You can decide which is more probable.

# 4

# GIANTS AND HEROES

Britain is a land awash with numerous stories of giants, such as the famous Gog and Magog giants defeated by Brutus and Corin in Cornwall. Also Wade and his wife, who built the castles at Mulgrave and Pickering by tossing a hammer between the two; the Wrekin giant from Wales who hated the people of Shrewsbury and wished to flood the town, but couldn't find it; and the Alphin and Alderman giants who fought over a beautiful water nymph and created large hills in the peaks by throwing great boulders at each other, plus many more. Of course many of us have seen the Cerne Abbas giant, whose colossal outline can still be viewed etched into the hillside in Dorset, holding aloft his club; but did giants really exist?

Local writer Daniel Codd tells of the skeleton of a 'true giant' that was unearthed in 1931 under Haxey High Street in Lincolnshire – a 7-foot tall man, thought to have been a Roman soldier.[1]

Lincolnshire has its fair share of giant folklore; oftentimes heroes whose epic deeds have elevated them to the status of giant.

There is a legend of a heroic fisherman, named Grim, after whom the Lincolnshire town of Grimsby is supposedly named. Although dismissed by many throughout the ages as a mere fairy tale, the story was very popular, especially in the eleventh century until around the time of Elizabeth I, with many claims that its roots were firmly based in fact. One of the earliest surviving written records alluding to the legend is a poem believed to have been created during the twelfth century, 'The Lai d' Haveloc'. The poet does, however, claim his poem is inspired from an older source and another writer claimed he used the sixth-century monk, Gildas, as his source, possibly dating the story back as far as AD 500.

According to the tale, during an invasion in Denmark the Danish King, Birabegn, was killed and the usurper, Godard, apparently ordered Grim to drown his boy, Havelok, the true heir to the Danish throne. Grim disobeyed and escaped with Havelok on a ship bound for England, eventually landing and settling along the Lincolnshire waters, making his living as a fisherman. He brought Havelok up as his own son and told no one, not even Havelok, of the boy's true heritage.

Havelok grew into an extremely tall and strong young man, yet kind and just – a true gentle giant. He would help his father sell and distribute fish, his great strength enabling him to carry vast amounts; more than double any other man could lift. As he grew older he found employment as a scullion to the Earl of Lincoln, where he became famous for his aptitude at sports. At stone-throwing contests it was always Havelok who managed to lift the heaviest stones and throw them further than anyone else. One such boulder he is said to have thrown can today be seen at the Welholme Galleries, aptly named the Havelok Stone.

> Then Havelok bent to raise the stone...I saw his mighty limbs harden and knot under the strain, and up to his knee he heaved it, and to his middle, and yet higher, to his chest...and then with a mighty lift it was at his shoulder, and he poised it...then hurled it from him...[a] full four paces beyond the strong porter's cast it flew, lighting with a mighty crash, and bedding itself in the ground.[2]

The Havelok Stone can be found within the grounds of the Welholme Galleries, Grimsby. The site is an old church, situated along the B1213, Welholme Road, between Hainton Avenue and Intax Mews.

News of Havelok's great might soon reached the ears of Earl Godrich, who had as his ward Goldborough, daughter of the late King Athelwold. Once of age, Godrich had promised to marry Goldborough to the strongest man in the land. Athelwold, obviously meant a king or prince, but Godrich took this opportunity to marry her off to the servant lad Havelok, therefore ensuring his own son would be heir to the throne instead of her. The two were forced to marry, both resenting the fact bitterly, but fate was to thwart Godrich, as Westwood explains:

> ...one night she [Goldborough] saw a light shining from her husband's mouth as he lay asleep. She saw, too, a cross on his shoulder, which the voice of an angel explained was the mark of a king, prophesying that Havelok would rule both England and Denmark.[3]

After questioning Grim about this secret and discovering the truth, Havelok and his new wife travelled to Denmark and overthrew Godard, Havelok claiming his rightful throne as king. Then they invaded England and defeated Godrich, apparently burning him to death. Havelok became King of England as well as Denmark, thus fulfilling the prophecy. It is told that Havelok and Goldborough lived happily ever after with their fifteen children and ruled together for sixty years.

The old seal of Grimsby depicts this tale, showing Grim as the central figure, the founder of Grimsby, with his sword and shield at the ready to defend the boy, Havelok, and the town. The hand of providence hangs above him, guiding his actions. On either side of him are Havelok and Goldborough, their crowns suspended above them indicating their royal standing. A mosaic of the seal decorates the outside wall of the Grimsby Central Library, a grand sight, except for the disabled ramp which unfortunately covers the bottom of the creation.

There is another legend of a kind-hearted Lincolnshire giant, Tom Hickathrift, whose abode was in the marshland around the Wash. Possibly of Saxon descent, he was described as a huge fellow possessing considerable strength. Polly Howat claims that at the start, Tom was rather a lazy fellow and that all he did was sit around the fire at home and eat all day, much to the exasperation of his poor, widowed mother.[4] She says that at just ten years of age he was already a 6-foot tall giant, 3 feet wide, eating as much as five normal men. He did posses great strength though; he allegedly kicked a football so hard that no one could ever find it.

One day a local farmer offered Tom's mother some fresh straw for her mattresses and told Tom to come and collect as much straw as he could carry. The poor farmer was soon eating his words, as Tom reluctantly followed him and came home with most of the field upon his back. Soon people from far and wide knew of his strength and he was eventually bribed into taking a job with a brewer, who had him trekking twenty miles across the marshes every day with a cart load of beer.

The Grimsby seal mosaic at the entrance of the Grimsby Central Library.

Tilney All Saints remembers Tom Hickathrift's victory by depicting his immense frame on their village sign.

The *Lincolnshire Life* magazine tells of a second giant who was living in another area of marshland and was terrorising all the locals and anyone who happened to pass through.[5] He would rob them and strike fear into everyone's heart. One day, Tom Hickathrift decided to take his cart over this area as a shortcut. The giant tried to attack him and Tom defended himself by rapidly removing the wheel and axle from the cart and using them as a club and shield. The two giants had a ferocious fight and Tom overcame his assailant, cutting off his head and leaving the villagers forever freed from his domination. Tom was labelled a hero and it is said he was called on from near and far to fight other giants who were causing trouble. Eventually he was apparently knighted for his good deeds and given the land of the first giant he fought, where he built a comfortable home for himself and his mother. Howat adds that he donated some of his land to the poor, on which they built a church dedicated to St James, as it was on the feast day of this saint that Tom had originally killed the giant.

There is another version, narrated on the fascinating website of Mike Burgess,[6] which he apparently sourced from a 1631 publication, *Ancient Funerall Monuments* [sic] by John Weever. This account concurs that Tom was working for a King's Lynn brewer and that it was while he was driving his cart of beer across the marshland that he came upon a heated

Possibly the final resting place of the giant Tom Hickathrift, a large tomb-like stone, now placed just outside the east door of the Tilney All Saints' Church.

dispute between the inhabitants thereof and their landlord. Tom supposedly saw that the common people's liberties were being infringed and felt such outrage that he tore the axel from his cart and saw off the landlord and his men, leaving the inhabitants free to enjoy their land. It seems unclear as to whether this was the original version of events or if, in fact, there really had been a vicious ogre terrorising the people. Either way Tom was classed a hero, with many ensuing adventures. He was said eventually to have teamed up with another huge chap, Henry Nonsuch, and together they defeated many foes.

As in many other legends, not least that of Robin Hood, there is a story that Tom himself determined where he should be buried when his time came to go. He threw a stone from his house, which is said to have landed just to the east of Tilney All Saints' churchyard. Here, an unmarked 8-foot stone slab lies at right angles with the pathway – perhaps the place Tom is now buried (especially if he shrunk a little in death!).

Around 300 years ago, a Wild Man of the Woods is said to have been spotted in the then heavily forested area around Stainfield. Myths of the Wild Man of the Wood, also known as the Woodwose, abound all over Europe – an ancient mythological figure; a huge, hairy man known to dwell amongst the trees; a guardian of the forests, not dissimilar to the Green Man – therefore it is not surprising that his appearance should also grace Lincolnshire.

The story tells that the Lincolnshire Wild Man of the Wood was creating rather a nuisance, killing locals and their livestock and so a gentleman named Francis Tyrwhitt-Drake is said to have tracked him down and dispatched him. Daniel Codd relates this tale, adding that there were other reasons this story could have come about and other explanations for his appearance on the Tyrwhitt-Drake coat of arms.[7] However, he does add that in the church in Bigby there is a monument to Sir Robert Tyrwhitt, depicting a giant hairy man lying across his feet – possibly indicating more truth to the story than first believed.

Monument to Sir Robert Tyrwhitt in Bigby Church, with the Wild Man of the Woods, who he apparently defeated, lying at his feet.

The pub sign of the Tyrwhitt Arms at Short Ferry depicting the wild man.

The Tyrwhitt Arms at Short Ferry certainly likes the tale, true or not, and have included the Wild Man, as depicted on the Tyrwhitt-Drake arms, on its pub sign!

Codd tells of the giant from the Isle of Axholme, William of Lindholme, who was a farmer's son.[8] The tale implies that the big lad was taken advantage of by his father, who would abuse the boy's extraordinary strength, making him do all the work around the farm by himself. William naturally resented this and made a few attempts to kill his parents. On one occasion he hurled a boulder into Wroot, where his parents had gone to a party, but his attempt to crush them failed, the rock landing past the house where they were. When they arrived home they reprimanded him severely, not only for trying to kill them, but also for leaving the fields unattended, where the sparrows could attack the crops freely. William replied that he had in fact caught all the sparrows and locked them in the barn, before he attempted murder. On inspection, his parents found this to be true, discovering the barn full of dead or dying sparrows, those left alive having turned entirely white with the shock. They were freed and apparently went on to form a colony of rare white sparrows in the area! Polly Howat adds that it took six strong horses to try and shift the boulder William had thrown, but even then the task was beyond them and the beasts fell down dead from exhaustion. Whispers that the stone was cursed began to spread and it was decided it should be left undisturbed.

> ...no ones da-ares so much as ter touch the stoo-an, or ter ra-ise it noo, though its nearly gressed o'er. If ever it should get gressed o'er, then, th' earth'll be covered wi' blood! No moss'll grow on t' stoo-an, for stoo-an eats it off as fast as it grows.[9]

According to Howat's source in 1976, someone did move the stone but within two years the person suffered a tragic bereavement in his family, the locals putting the misfortune down to the curse. Gutch and Peacock add that there were two other immense boulders within the vicinity, thought to have been brought there by William, called the Thumb Stone and the Little Finger Stone.[10]

William's reputation was somewhat tarnished due to these attempts to kill his family and rumours spread that he was in league with the Devil. Even his colossal strength was attributed to selling his soul to Satan. Like Tom Hickathrift, there is the same story which illustrates his strength, whereby he was able to rope an amazing amount of hay to his back and carry it home for his mattress.

Codd relates how, when the locals wanted to build a causeway through the marshes, from Hatfield Moors to Wroot, William boasted he would complete the road single-handedly and at record speed, on the condition that no one could watch him work. William was allowed to begin the task and a local horseman rode before him to show him the required route. This horseman knew the conditions William had set but could not resist a glance behind him to see what the giant was doing. His eyes nearly popped out of his head as he saw William speeding along behind him, surrounded by a haze of flying gravel, stones and pebbles as he made the track. Yet the most shocking sight was that of hundreds and hundreds of tiny demons in little red coats, intermingled in the haze, helping the giant as he worked.

Terrified, the horseman allegedly whispered a prayer to God and urged his horse to go faster to escape the horrors behind him. William knew, however, that the horseman had gone against his word and ceased his work immediately. All the imps disappeared and the causeway was never finished.

Stories of the giant's death were also allegedly linked to the Devil. Having sold his soul to him, Satan obviously knew when William's time was up and consequently, the giant prepared his grave very carefully. He dug his own hole then propped a huge flagstone next to it. When the Devil came for him William lay himself down in his hole and batted away the pole holding up the flagstone. The stone crashed down, entombing the giant and he was never seen again – although his tales lived on long after.

Codd writes that in the 1930s, folklorist Ethel Rudkin was told of a hermitage that existed in the 1700s, which was believed to have been where William lived. Apparently a large flagstone was discovered at this site and when excavated some human bones of a very large skeleton were found. Rudkin's source suggested that those bones were now kept in an old box in the granary at Lindholme Hall, Hatfield but when enquiring I was told that this was no longer the case. Unfortunately, the flagstone, which originally had some kind of inscription engraved upon it, was broken up and so Rudkin never discovered what it had said.

Adrian Gray relates the tale of another giant who lived in Lincolnshire a long time ago.[11] This giant was so tall that he literally had his head in the clouds! He was, however, as is often the case with these legendary giants, rather stupid and clumsy. Fortunately, his best friend, a very small dwarf, was extremely clever and also very good. The two of them would always travel round together, the dwarf living in his friend's pocket and helping him out with the difficulties in life. On this particular occasion, the two of them had been for a very long walk in the countryside and the fresh air had given them both a huge appetite. As they walked the dwarf suddenly pointed out a succulent looking flock of sheep grazing on a nearby field. Being rather a moralistic dwarf, however, he expressed his unease at killing and eating someone else's sheep without asking permission, but as they were both so hungry he decided they would eat first then find the owner later and repay him by doing some work. The giant was so strong, after all, that he could do the work of twenty men in half the time, with the direction of his friend, the dwarf.

The dwarf gave a loud whistle, calling his other dwarf friends from round about to come and join the feast. Together they caught a small lamb and sat down to eat, while the giant helped himself to two large rams, as his appetite matched his stature!

They all enjoyed a delicious dinner but just as they were finishing off the last scraps of meat, they spotted a wizard walking along the lane towards them. This wizard was the owner of the sheep they had just killed and eaten, and as fortune would have it he was rather a mean and malicious man, who would not be pleased with what he found. The dwarfs all scattered, hiding in the hillside, and our clever dwarf dived back inside the giant's pocket. The giant, however, was too big and too stupid to hide and so was still left sitting in the field surrounded by the bones of the meal they had just finished when the wizard arrived. Spying the carcasses laid all around, the wizard flew into a terrible rage: 'Who dares to kill my precious ram with the golden horns?' he bellowed.

The giant was at a loss as what to say, but the clever dwarf piped up from his hiding place in the pocket, making himself sound like the giant. Now the dwarf, being very good and noble, hated lying, but he was not the one who had killed the ram with the golden horns, so in fact he was telling the truth when he said, 'Not me,' even though the wizard thought it was the giant who was answering.

'Well, who has slaughtered my prize ram with the silver horns?' he demanded.

'Not me,' the dwarf replied again, truthfully.

'And who has killed my poor little curly lamb?' the wizard cried, glaring at the giant.

At this the dwarf was in a quandary, as he had actually been the one to kill this lamb and he really did not want to lie. Instead, he pinched the giant's skin hard, hoping that he would cotton on, and fortunately he did.

'Not me,' replied the giant, and even though the wizard was still suspicious he knew that no falsehood had been uttered. He decided to test the giant with a riddle to try and catch him out, promising another of his sheep as a prize if the riddle was answered correctly but ordering that the giant would have to serve him for one hundred years if he got the riddle wrong:

Cold feet, cold head
Brown, dry but not dead.
What am I?

The brainless giant had no idea, but the dwarf figured it out and answered, 'A tree in winter.' This was the correct answer, but before they were allowed to feast on their prize, they had to pose the wizard a riddle, with the same rules applying – if he was baffled they were free to eat the sheep and leave, if not the giant was his slave for a hundred years. The dwarf knew it had to be a good one and thought hard before eventually answering:

Two for one
A small one for the rest
And a little, little piece for my pocket.

The riddle, of course, referred to the meal they had just had and as the wizard had no idea what had happened to his sheep, he couldn't know the answer to the puzzle. He became extremely angry but knew he had been out-done and so departed in rather a huff.

The other dwarfs came out of their hiding holes and joined in the new feast but the daft giant became carried away in the excitement and carried on eating all the other sheep and an ox as well. The wizard had been watching from afar and returned full of fury. 'Well, who has eaten my ox?' he shouted, knowing full well it was the giant. 'Not me,' the silly giant replied, remembering his line from earlier, but this time he was lying and the spell was cast to enslave him to the wizard's service for a hundred years!

Gray goes on to explain that one of the tasks the wizard made the poor giant perform was to dig up some of the hills in Yorkshire and plant them along the Trent riverside, thus helping stop the annual flood that threatened the villages. The river was very cross about this and every year after that it created a huge wave to try and overcome the flood barriers, to no avail – yet that wave can still be seen every so often, even now.

One cannot possibly talk about the folklore and tales of Lincolnshire, never mind its giants and heroes, without mentioning Hereward the Wake. Depicted as both a giant and a hero, the stories of Hereward are a mixture of fact and fiction, the written accounts being of dubious reliability. Overall, however, he is remembered as an Anglo-Saxon rebel leader, fighting against King William I's Norman regime during the eleventh century. Even though the tales often elevate Hereward to giant stature, there seems to only be one written account that describes his appearance, and in this account he is short! Peter Rex quotes from the *Gesta Herewardi*, 'Short, stoutly made, agile, with long golden hair, an oval face, with eyes light in colour and not matched.'[12]

Rex goes on to state that, 'Among his other, non-military, talents was the ability to sing and play the harp "after the manner of the Girvii" – that is the tribe called the Gyrwe living on the western edge of the Fens and from whom the Fenlanders were descended.'

Sources state that Hereward was the son of Leofric of Bourne and his wife Aediva, although the Domesday Book does not show that Hereward ever held

Bourne, nor can a reference to any Leofric of Bourne be found. There is a Leofric who held land in Lincolnshire and elsewhere in 1066 but there is no proof that he was connected with Hereward. Rex believes that many of the older historical accounts tend to embellish certain facts in order to give them more weight and that their philosophy was often along the lines of 'heroes need illustrious ancestors'.[13] With this in mind, we must remember that certain parts of the Hereward story, although based in fact, do tend towards legend, but for our purposes that only makes for better reading!

Hereward was either exiled or fled around 1063, when he was eighteen; some sources saying his father persuaded King Edward to make him an outlaw as he was keeping very bad company then and causing trouble fighting and stealing, although prior to this he seems to have been a man of some means, owning much land around Lincolnshire. He had many adventures whilst exiled, with his trusty companion Martin Lightfoot, and some sources say he made his way to Northumbria, where the exile laws did not carry much weight. It is said he lived and trained with his godfather, Gilbert of Ghent, who had in his possession an incredibly strong, large white polar bear.[14] The bear was kept in a cage and also had one leg chained down for added security, but the story tells that one day it escaped and Hereward found it in the courtyard about to rush at a petrified young girl. Without hesitation, he sprang into action and brought his battleaxe down hard upon the skull of the bear. The bear fell dead just in front of the stunned girl and Hereward's fight with the beast became a renowned folk tale.

Legend sends Hereward on various romantic adventures, around Northumbria, Ireland, Flanders and in another heroic story he ends up in Cornwall. It is here he is said to have rescued the daughter of the reputed King of Cornwall from marrying a man she was not in love with and reuniting her with the King of Ireland's son, whom she wanted to marry. Hereward, the true heroic knight!

It was while he was travelling round during his exile that he heard his homeland had become 'subject to the rule of foreigners'[15] and that the Normans had seized his father's estates and murdered his younger brother. He returned to England with his bride, Turfrida, and planned how to retake his father's house. Marlow writes that he placed himself one night at the gate of the house and listened to the revelry and drunkenness within.[16] A lady inside tried to calm the foreigners by telling them the brother may come and exact revenge for those they had murdered. The French laughed at her and said he would not dare show his face, and at this Hereward revealed himself and slew every last one of them. He took his revenge for his fallen brother, whose head greeted him on a spike by the door on his return home and legend states that fourteen Norman heads replaced it above the door the next day. This defeat of the Normans caused word to spread and English and Danish warriors to gather with him to form an alliance against the Norman Conquest.

Hereward and his followers are said to have made their hideouts in the Fens, wetlands and marshes, which were then also thickly forested in parts, giving his

The Aldreth village sign remembers Hereward, as the area is thought to have been a causeway into the Isle of Ely and it was also possibly the site of two battles fought by Hereward.

story a Robin Hood feel. They knew the treacherous marshes by heart and so were hidden from the enemy and had the advantage.

> Vast areas of the original Fenland were once totally untamed marsh and Fen consisting of deep pools, sheets of open water, and copses of alder and willow. Through it ran streams and rivers among reed beds and stands of rush and sedge. It abounded in wildlife; and all those who went there were exposed to the often unwelcome attentions of those who had chosen a wild life.[17]

This suited Hereward and his men and they joined the stronghold on the Isle of Ely, which was surrounded by this Fenland and which William the Conqueror wished to take. The Isle of Ely was an ideal place for a stronghold – access across bridges could be easily guarded and it was easy to pick off approaching forces, especially strangers unfamiliar with the land who, dressed in heavy armour, would struggle in the unstable marshes. Fire in the marshes could also spread quickly as the sedge and reed were extremely flammable and this terrified the opposing army. The abundance of wildlife in the area made a siege work in their favour as they had plenty of food and water to keep them alive.

The siege is said to have lasted six years, with King William trying different tactics to overthrow Ely. First, after creating a blockade around the Isle guarding all known exits, he decided to create a causeway of masses of alder branches overlaying the reeds, with stones, sticks and huge timbers lashed together. However, Hereward and his men were lying in wait and ambushed William's attempts, destroying the causeway and killing hundreds of his men, many others being sucked down into the marshes in their heavy armour and drowning. It is said that many years passed before the Fen-men ceased dragging up bodies of those Normans who had sunk into the depths that day.

While William was regrouping, legend states that Hereward ventured out, getting past the enemy defences and disguised himself as a potter, in order to glean the plans of the Normans. He penetrated the enemy camp and discovered they were planning to use a witch against him but later he was recognised and had to fight his way out, relying on his trusty stead, Swallow, to get him away from trouble. He managed to get back to Ely with important information about the new attack and began to put a plan together to foil it.

The king employed a series of boats in his next attack and also built up mounds for soldiers to fight upon and towers from which he could deploy

Ely Cathedral Abbey.

catapults and other weapons. It was upon one of these towers that the witch was mounted and began to utter her spells and incantations, to provoke and scare the rebels.

Hereward and his men had, however, been infiltrating the enemy lines, disguised as fishermen, and it was now that they threw off their disguises and set fire to all the platforms, mounds and towers. The Normans who survived the flames are said to have fled in terror and the witch fell from her collapsing, fiery tower and broke her neck. Hereward and his men picked off any remaining survivors and thus triumphed over the Normans yet again.

It would seem that the siege could have lasted a good many more years, with who knows what outcome, if Hereward had not been betrayed. The monks of Ely were growing tired of the siege and wished to win the king's favour. Abbot Thurstan made a pact with the king and showed his army a secret way across the Fens. Hereward and his men were surprised by this attack and thousands were killed or captured but the story goes that Hereward himself managed to escape, guided through the marshes by a mysterious white wolf.

The facts become even more clouded from here. Hereward seems to have continued his rebellion, attacking the Normans whenever he could, sacking Peterborough and Stamford and eventually being caught and imprisoned. Another story tells that he made his peace with the king and lived side by side with him ever after, with his new wife, Alftrude. Yet another states that he met his end when he was set upon one night by a band of Normans. He apparently managed to slay fifteen or sixteen of them single-handedly, but then was stabbed in the back by another four who came in from behind.

Rex believes that each of the differing medieval stories stemming from the Fenland monasteries had a different perspective to show, with varying priorities about how Hereward should be viewed, and so this is one reason why the facts of what happened to him are so unclear.

No one really knows the ultimate fate of this heroic Englishman and thus he melds into the realm of legend, but is forever remembered as a champion of English liberty!

# 5

# THINGS THAT GO BUMP IN THE LINCOLNSHIRE NIGHT

I include a chapter on ghosts and hauntings because throughout the centuries they have always held a certain amount of fascination for people from all walks of life. Indeed today, producers now use ghost-hunting programmes as a form of 'reality television', but the majority of ghost stories originate from the past and many are closely linked with folk history. As the second largest county in England, covering nearly 6,000 square kilometres, Lincolnshire is destined to be inundated with legends of ghosts, phantoms and unexplained occurrences. Like all the counties on this historical island, Lincolnshire has its fair share of castles, churches, cathedrals, stately homes, abbeys and historical sites, many of which claim their own particular brand of haunting.

Not only one of the most famous hauntings of Lincolnshire but also one of the most famous cases of suspected poltergeist activity in Britain occurred in 1716 and 1717 at Epworth Rectory, situated in the Isle of Axholme. The Reverend Samuel Wesley and his family, including John and Charles Wesley, the founders of Methodism, owned the house at the time.

It was the children and servants who first began to complain of hearing knocking sounds in the house, accompanied by peculiar groans and mysterious footsteps at all hours of the night. One of the children identified one sound as the tread of a man's heavy leather boots. The reverend, however, heard no such noises and reprimanded the children for such fabrications, until a few nights later he finally heard loud thuddings against his own bedchamber wall. At first he believed that someone had entered the house and was causing trouble. This would not have been so far-fetched as, back in 1709, disgruntled villagers who did not agree with his stern principles had set his house on fire. Some livestock had been injured and the rectory had to undergo some building work to repair it, but no one was hurt. However, it transpired that no one was anywhere near the rectory on this particular night.

The following is an extract taken from a letter Mrs Wesley wrote to her absent son, Samuel, to inform him of the strange goings on:

> On the first of December our maid heard, at the door of the dining-room, several dismal groans, like a person in extremes, at the point of death. We gave little heed to her relation, and endeavoured to laugh her out of her fears. Some nights (two or three) after, several of the family heard a strange knocking in divers places, usually three or four knocks at a time, and then stayed a little. This continued every night for a fortnight; sometimes it was in the garret, but most commonly in the nursery, or green chamber. We all heard it but your father, and I was not willing he should be informed of it, lest he should fancy it was against his own death, which, indeed, we all apprehended. But when it began to be troublesome, both day and night, that few or none of the family durst be alone, I resolved to tell him of it, being minded he should speak to it. At first he would not believe but somebody did it to alarm us; but the night after, as soon as he was in bed, it knocked loudly nine times, just by his bedside. He rose, and went to see if he could find out what it was, but could see nothing. Afterwards he heard it as the rest.[1]

To counter any more untoward behaviour, the reverend bought a guard dog, but the first night the imposing beast heard the knocking he fled whimpering behind his master's legs. Glasses were heard smashing, windows broken and Mrs Wesley even heard the sound of a bag of coins being emptied at her feet. Even though the bangs and crashes were demonstrably noisy and the family searched every room in the house, there was no-one to be found, nothing untoward to be seen.

One night, when the knockings were particularly loud on the nursery door, the reverend lost his temper and shouted at the spectre to leave the children alone and bother him instead. The spectre obliged and directly came knocking on his study door. The reverend also reported being pushed by an unseen force in his study. Even the clergyman they called in to help fled the house in fear after a rather raucous show!

Eventually the children became accustomed to the presence and nicknamed him 'Old Jeffery'. One of the daughters claimed to have actually seen him once – a man in a long, trailing, white robe – while others asserted they had seen some animal creature appearing as a badger, rat or even a white rabbit, scuttling under their beds. Perhaps the strangest thing about the whole incident is that it apparently stopped as abruptly as it had started, with no explanation as to who or what had been the cause. Suggestions include witchcraft, the curse of an unhappy marriage, the daughters' development into womanhood, and Jacobite grumblings – but the reverend had his own theory. The story tells that one night at prayer, the reverend noticed his wife did not say 'Amen' at the end of the prayer for the king. When questioned on this matter, she said she refused on the grounds that the Prince of Orange was no king. The reverend then

The Old Rectory at Epworth, the home of John Wesley and the poltergeist Old Jeffery.

vowed he would not live with her again until she retracted this and he left the house for a year. When he returned, she apparently had still not taken it back, so when the knockings and bangings began, the reverend believed it was due to him breaking his vow, which had not been forgotten by God.

The actual term 'poltergeist' originates from the German *poltern*, which means to knock or break, and *geist* which translates as spirit, or ghost. Generally poltergeist activity starts and stops very abruptly, which is one of the reasons it was believed Epworth Rectory had been visited by one, rather than a demon or any other type of ghost. The Old Rectory is now open to the public as a museum to the life and works of the Wesley brothers, so you can visit yourself and walk in the footsteps of Old Jeffery.

Folklorist Ethel Rudkin mentions more Lincolnshire poltergeist activity happening at Owmby Abbey, near Caistor (now replaced by cottages). She relates the tale of a man who was passing by when he saw a woman who had fainted. She was:

> ...laid in' the causey, an' she'd fainted wi' fright, on account of 'er 'avin' been sittin' in the room with one o' the childer when there started such a din! In the corner cupboard the teaspoons was all put away in the milk-jug – well – they all started tittuppin' – then, woosh! Down when the blind, an' she screamed an' 'id 'er face. When she looked up, blind wasn't down at all, it was up![2]

Another episode tells of the kitchen fire lighting itself and people hearing it crackling, but when they looked again there was no fire lit.

Local researcher Daniel Codd recounts a poltergeist haunting a house in Leasingham, near Sleaford, in 1679.[3] Occurrences included the latch on the door jiggling of its own accord, doors slamming, phantom footsteps and knockings and chairs gathering by themselves and then returning to their proper places in the house. Codd adds that this particular poltergeist had the strange habit of copying sounds it heard around the house, such as workmen banging, or servants breaking coals, but would repeat them during the evening, when the workmen had gone home.

Codd also tells of a poltergeist-like haunting at the Old Rectory at Fulletby, near Horncastle. He explains that during the 1800s some renovations were being made to the building, during which time an old skull was found. It was buried in the churchyard but the following morning it was discovered amongst the builders' rubble. It was again buried in the churchyard but the unexplained excavation was repeated the following morning. In the end the superstitious builders walled the skull up in the chimney place of the new building. The poltergeist activity started following these events. Loud banging and smashing sounds were heard. Servants reported waking in the middle of the night to find their bed sheets had been stripped and thrown across the room. In 1840 the house had more renovations and the chimney was demolished. This brought an end to the poltergeist haunting.

Rudkin describes an exorcism to rid the Manor Farm at East Halton of a ghost, another possible poltergeist, although she indicates the haunting might have been connected with monks who used to live there. So disturbing were the events that occurred that the only apparent solution was to trap the evil spirit in an iron pot and keep it in the cellar. The occupants of the house were told not to move the pot, for fear of bad luck – and certainly not to open it, as the spirit would be let loose once again.

Another incident of a spirit being captured in an iron pot occurred at Normanby-by-Spital. The legend tells that it took twelve parsons to lay this spirit, who was said to be very obnoxious and vindictive. They apparently asked what it wanted and it replied 'Life I want, life I'll have'.[4] So the parsons threw it a live cock which, it is claimed, was torn limb from limb and devoured. This caused the distraction the parsons needed and whilst it was busy with the cock, they lowered the iron pot over it, which was then somehow pushed into the ground. It seems that spirits do not like iron! They say that placing an iron rod across a grave will prevent ghosts from rising out of the ground and an iron horseshoe at the entrance to a building will stop ghosts from coming in. With this in mind, let us hope both iron pots work, especially for the sake of the present-day inhabitants there!

As well as poltergeist activity, Lincolnshire has many a poor ghost, victims of none other than love – unrequited love, love lost, love turned to hatred and thwarted love. Love has a lot to answer for!

The ghost of Tom Otter is perhaps one of the better known Lincolnshire ghosts. His was a simple tale of a young man and woman falling in love. It was 1800 when

The Sun Inn, Saxilby, where Tom Otter was tried for the murder of his wife and where poor Mary Kirkham's spirit still roams. Above the fireplace, where the murder weapon was once kept, is a photograph of how the inn used to look and some information regarding the story.

he travelled to Lincoln looking for work and met the fair Mary Kirkham. They courted and soon she became pregnant. Her father demanded Tom either marry the girl or go to jail, so he kept quiet about the fact that he was already a married man and married Mary in 1805. However, the next day Mary's body was found in a lane; she had been murdered with a hedge stake. Tom, of course, was arrested and went on trial at the Sun Inn, Saxilby. Mary's body was also taken there and her blood, which was said to have spilled onto the steps, stained them for many years afterwards, despite vigorous attempts to clean it away. The room where her body was placed is said to be haunted by the cries of a new-born baby.

Tom was hanged and then his body, fastened in an iron cage, was hung up high for everyone to see. It is said the body fell down twice, due to the weight of the iron, and the second time it killed a man.

The murder weapon was kept above the fireplace at the Sun Inn but every year on the anniversary of the murder, it was mysteriously moved, although the inn was locked and the weapon securely fastened with iron strapping or staples. On each occasion, it was discovered at the murder site, covered in what appeared to be fresh blood. There used to be a saying in Lincoln when ordering a new rope or chain required to be very strong: 'Ma'ke it strong enough to hold Tom Otter's hedge stake.'

The stake was eventually burned by the Bishop of Lincoln in the hope that the ghost would be laid to rest. The lane where Mary was found is now called Tom Otters Lane (the B1190) and his body was left hanging there until a storm in 1850 blew what remained of the gibbet down. Some say that part of the gibbet was taken to be displayed at Doddington Hall.

His body had been on public display for so long that he had become quite famous, notwithstanding the eerie incidents that also drew the crowds. When his body was old and rotting, birds would make nests in his skull and there was a rhyme that existed even after his gibbet fell:

There were nine tongues within one head;
The tenth went out to seek for bread;
To feed the living within the dead.[5]

With all the mysterious happenings surrounding this story some people have speculated as to whether Tom was the real murderer or perhaps just the scapegoat? Could this be why there was so much unrest in the spirit world regarding the murder of Mary Kirkham?

Gainsborough Old Hall is one site of many with a ghost that harbours a broken heart. The Grey Lady is this particular phantom, who has been seen on numerous occasions floating along the corridors with her long dress swishing beneath her. She frequents the East Wing corridor near the tower and disappears into the wall. Apparently, during some renovations in the 1940s, part of the wall in that corridor was stripped back and a doorway was found beneath it. Legend states this is the doorway the Grey Lady comes through, looking for her forbidden lover. As daughter of Lord of the Manor, she was not allowed to marry her soldier sweetheart and when her father discovered plans for an elopement he exiled her to the tower where she pined away her years, nursing her broken heart.

William Rose, after whom Roses Trentside Albion Works is named, spent much of his childhood in the 1800s at the Old Hall. He is said to have encountered the Grey Lady during this period, a tale that he told, even in his late years, with such detail that it must have made quite an impression on him. She has become an attraction at the house now and her spirit is said still to wander.

Gunby Hall boasts a similar, if somewhat more gruesome, story. Sir William Massingberd had the hall built for himself in 1700 after a regrettable incident. His daughter, Margaret, unfortunately fell passionately in love with one of his postilion riders who rode the lead horse on her father's coach, an affair of which Massingberd thoroughly disapproved. The lovers attempted a secret elopement but were discovered, and in a furious temper Massingberd shot the rider dead and hid his body in the pond. Some versions say he also shot his daughter and threw them both in. The path near the pond is now known as the Ghost Walk, for this is where the lovers are reputed to walk for eternity, not to be parted even by death. Alfred Lord Tennyson enjoyed spending time at Gunby Hall, describing it as 'a haunt of ancient peace', and now a

Gainsborough Old Hall, open to the public, is a fascinating building to visit. Each part of the structure has been built at differing time periods and in varying styles.

Gunby Hall, near Spilsby; open to the public.

The Ghost Walk in the grounds of Gunby Hall, along the side of the carp pond, on the way to the church. This is where the ghosts of the lovers are said to be seen.

National Trust property it is certainly worth a visit, as the grounds are indeed a haven, if you avoid crossing the lovers!

Rudkin describes another lovelorn tragedy that occurred at Fillingham Castle:

> But the castle itself is 'aunted – because a man as once lived there cut 'is throat or else shot 'isself on the front door step, an' all along of a lady's 'avin' jilted 'im; an' at night 'is spirit 'aunts the great long corridors because 'e can't rest.[6]

However, another report states that a Green Lady haunts the castle, the ghost of a girl who committed suicide after her beloved left her.

Harmston Hall,[7] near Waddington, holds a mystery that has never been satisfactorily explained. The story tells that during the time of George IV, the family in residence at the hall suddenly departed one night, never to return. When the hall was opened some thirty years later to have an inventory taken, the dining room was found exactly as it had been the evening the family left, except for a film of dust and cobwebs, not unlike Miss Havisham's wedding banquet. Chairs were apparently lying where they had been bowled over, wine glasses had been knocked on the floor in the rush to leave – there was even wine left in the decanters. Something quite terrifying must have happened for them to flee in such a manner. Officially, people said that the squire had just found out his wife had been having an affair with his best friend. He had sent everyone away that very hour and locked up the house, then left. Strangely neither the wife nor the friend were ever seen again and rumour spread that they had been murdered and buried under the hearth in that very room.

Years later, a gentleman farmer took the hall but he and his family claimed it was terribly haunted. Screams would be heard every night and the sounds of a fight or struggle. Footsteps running along the passage and the sound of a body falling against a door were common occurrences. No family ever stayed very long in that house, and in 1930 it became part of a new mental health hospital complex. This complex, as you can imagine, had its fair share of supernatural happenings and was finally closed down in 1990. Since then, it was redeveloped to become a private home again. One wonders what disturbances, if any, remain.

The Irby Boggle is reputed to haunt Irby Dale Woods. In 1455, Rosamund Guy and Neville Randell, who were betrothed, allegedly met for a romantic tryst in the woods the night before their wedding. Apparently the rendezvous turned into a violent quarrel and ended in the murder of Rosamund, although her body was not found. The story states that no one saw them after they went for their walk, but people from the village heard their shouting and speculation grew. Rosamund's father swore that justice for his daughter must be done, or else her ghost would haunt Irby Dale Wood for 500 years.

Witnesses have seen a spirit in what is believed to be a white wedding dress, walking in the woods, and legend states that many years later some workmen uncovered the skeleton of a woman underneath the branches of an oak into which, as lovers, they had carved their initials. What the argument was about

The reputedly haunted Harmston Hall, Waddington. This is now a private house.

Irby Dale Woods is a large and picturesque wood to visit. There is a small car park by the road at Irby upon Humber and then a fairly long walk to the trees across farmland, but the public path is well maintained.

Bradley Woods, furnished with car parking facilities, is a pretty nature reserve well worth a visit, even if you see nothing of the Black Lady!

no one ever knew, but Neville was never brought to justice for his actions, leaving Rosamund's ghost to wander the woods for 500 years.

Bradley Woods is another Lincolnshire wood that is reputedly haunted. It is here that the ghost of the Black Lady roams, searching for her lost love and the baby that was snatched away from her. She is said to be of average height, very pretty and wearing a long, flowing black cloak with a hood. Her face is ghostly pale and grief-stricken but although she is shocking to behold, she is said not to hurt anyone.

The story goes that she was a beautiful woman in life, happily married to a woodsman and living in a cottage in the woods. They had a baby together on whom they both doted, but one day the husband was called away to fight in the War of the Roses. The wife missed him terribly and pined for him, circling around the wood every day watching for him to return. One day, some enemy soldiers entered the woods and found her, alone and helpless. They assaulted her and stole her baby, leaving her with nothing. Half mad with sorrow, she wandered incessantly in search of her missing baby as well as her absent husband. She never saw either again and died of a broken heart. Her restless spirit continues to search for them still. The sightings of her were so common that mothers used to use her story to frighten their children: 'If yer don't stop yer awming the Black Lady'll get yer!'

There have been modern sightings of the Black Lady and some people have reported seeing the leaves on the path in front of them moving, as if someone were walking across them. There is also a myth that if you visit the wood on Christmas Eve and shout out to her 'Black Lady, Black Lady, I've stolen your baby!' three times, she will appear ready to rescue her child. This would be a heartless game, for the story is sad enough and one can only hope she may find peace.

There are more stories of hauntings connected with love, such as the Lady in Green, who is said to be seen in Thorpe Hall. When the owner of the hall, Sir John Bolle, was abroad in the 1500s, a Spanish lady fell in love with him and wanted to marry him. Unfortunately he already had a wife in England, so as a symbol of her love for him the Spanish girl gave him a picture of herself for him to take home. It would seem that her everlasting love for him was somehow caught up in the picture and her spirit has been seen wandering the hall ever since.

There is also a headless bride, which Fisk states haunts Scremby late at night;[8] rather a frightful sight, and one can only imagine what occurred on her wedding night!

Another is the story of a ghostly figure of a young woman, Sarah Preston, married to a local ship owner, who has been seen to jump from the Boston Stump tower, holding a baby in her arms, but then vanishing before hitting the ground. Legend states that in 1585, she had an affair with a sailor from whom she contracted the plague, which then infected the rest of the village, claiming the lives of hundreds of people in Boston. She was driven to suicide by the angry mob.

There is an alternative story about the ghostly figure seen to jump. The woman was thought to be happily married, yet lost her husband not long after giving birth to their child. She was so grief-stricken that she took the baby and threw herself off the Stump Tower, hoping for a reunion with her beloved. The lady is actually supposed to appear if you run around the Stump three times at the stroke of midnight.

The list for lovelorn ghosts could continue but there is a plethora of other ghostly happenings in Lincolnshire that also deserve a mention.

One rather strange ghostly apparition is that of a hare at Bolingbroke Castle. The castle is now a ruin but open to the public, so you can search for the hare yourself. It is a wily, timeless creature, evading capture by any means, as this extract from *The Gentleman's Magazine* in 1821 illustrates:

> One thinge is not to be passed by affirmed as a certaine trueth by many of the inhabitants of the towne upon their owne knowledge, which is, that the castle is haunted by a certain spirit in the likenesse of a hare; which att the meeting of the auditors doeth usually runne between their legs, and sometimes overthrows them, and soe passes away. They have pursued it downe into the castleyard, and seene it take in att a grate into a low cellar, and have followed it thither with a light, where notwithstanding that they did most narrowly observe it [and that there was noe other passage out, but by the doore, or windowe, the roome being all close framed of stones within, not having the least chinke or crevice] yet they could never finde it. And att other tymes it hath been seene run in at iron-grates below into other of the grotto's [as there be many of them] and they have watched the place, and sent for houndes and put in after it; but after a while they have come crying out.[9]

There have long been tales of hares throughout the world, with links to the moon and as creatures belonging to witchcraft or even disguised as witches. Ghost hunter Rod Collins[10] affirms that Bolingbroke Castle was once used to hold a witch and states that the apparition is her ghost.

There is the tale of another hare-like creature being seen along the road between Kirton and Grayingham, thought possibly to be a nineteenth-century haunting, based on the story of a murder that happened there. Rudkin presents the account of one B. Willoughton, who tells that a man named Copeman was murdered by one Trafford in this place, and Trafford is said to have laid the body out in the field by the edge of the lane. Since then, grass is supposedly never able to grow where Copeman's head and heels touched the ground.

> But there is something in the 'auntin' there…One night me an' a pal 'ad been to Kirton…we was bicyclin' back, an' when we got to that bit 'o road…there was a man a-'orse-back comin' at us up the road. Now, whether we went through 'im; or if we didn't, where 'e went to I don't know! But we came 'ome like greased lightnin' after that, I can tell yer!

Rudkin goes on to narrate the sighting of the hare-like creature running down this road: 'It was mostlins as big as an owd 'are, but with two 'orns an' only

The Boston Stump.

The picturesque ruin of Bolingbroke Castle, surrounded by ponds and greenery. It is well signposted and easily found.

two feet, an' its feet clattered on the road.'[11] This description sounds more like a devilish imp than a hare – perhaps it is just another manifestation of the ghostly presence, like the phantom horseman.

An additional animal spectre is that of a sow with piglets. In some legends, the sighting of a phantom sow with her litter was a sign that alms to the poor had not been paid. Once they were paid as they were supposed to be, the sightings stopped. It seems unlikely that this was the cause of this particular spectre, however, as she appeared regularly every Halloween along Bonnewells Lane, Bransby. Rudkin tells us the lane is badly haunted, with sightings of a Black Dog and also a lady with a rustling silk dress; an interesting place for a ghost hunter to visit!

At Gunthorpe, Commonpiece Lane, there have been numerous sightings of a large, white phantom cat. One story tells of a local man returning home on a snowy night when he saw the cat. He apparently kicked at it, and it vanished into thin air. The next morning he returned to the spot and as no more snow had fallen that night, his own footsteps could clearly be seen in the snow. He could even see where he had kicked out at the cat, but there were no traces whatsoever of the cat's paws. Legend states that human bones have been discovered in this place, although no answer was ever forthcoming as to who the unfortunate person was, nor how they met their demise. Ghost cats are a fairly common sighting, some believing them to linger where their loyalties once lay, as a kind of protector. This is one possible explanation for the ghost cat at Gunthorpe.

Moving away from animal spectres, Christopher Marlow regales us with the wonderful tale of the ghosts of All Saints' Church, at Holbeach. He tells of four firm friends who, in the late seventeenth century, regularly met at the Checquers to play cards into the early hours. Unfortunately, one of the four friends, farmer John Guymer, was struck down with a serious illness and died within in a few days. The other three were distraught at losing their card partner:

> 'Alas now we shall play no more' said one. 'Farmer Guymer is dead and there is no one to take his place.' 'Say not so...' answered the second. 'Let us drink confusion to the Devil who has fetched him and pray for another partner to join our game.'[12]

On the night of his funeral, the remaining men continued to drink and chatter late into the night, until they became so inebriated that they decided to go and visit their friend in the churchyard. One had the terrible suggestion of having a game of cards as of old, with their dead friend, and so they dug him up and all four entered the church ready to play. They propped old farmer Guymer against the rails and took it in turns to guide his hand in the game, jeering and bellowing every so often and having not a thought of reverence. They continued thus into the small hours, when suddenly there was a hideous booming laugh all around them. Their dead friend disappeared and in his place sat the Devil, who smiled as he uttered a warning for them to save themselves.

# THINGS THAT GO BUMP IN THE LINCOLNSHIRE NIGHT 103

The alleged haunted entrance to the All Saints' Church at Holbeach, where the ghosts beckon drunkards to their doom.

The effigy of Sir Humphrey Littlebury, who is thought to haunt All Saints' Church, Holbeach.

Then just as suddenly as he had appeared, he vanished and farmer Guymer was back in his stiff position. The three men convinced themselves it had been a trick of the light, a drunken hallucination. They continued to play, taunting the dead man for his game but alas, there was eventually a horrendous shriek and three grisly phantoms appeared and sped towards them. Each phantom seized a man, grabbing him tightly and then vanishing with him. Only poor farmer Guymer, left propped up against the rails, was found in the morning when the villagers ventured into the church to discover the source of the screams of the night before. Legend says a sly smile of victory played upon his lips. Forever afterwards, the villagers of Holbeach testified that the ghosts of the three men would stand in the doorway of the church at night, with the stiff corpse of their dead friend, 'and beckon all drunken men to their doom'.

Commenting on the story, Codd's research has shown the surnames of each man to be historically accurate, so the men did exist but their fate is unknown. He gives the explanation that the three men could have been heard making a din in the church that fateful night and were set upon by grave robbers or thieves, and thus met their end. As for shadows beckoning others to follow, you will have to make up your own mind.

These ghosts of Holbeach's All Saints' Church are said to share their haunting with the phantom of Sir Humphrey Littlebury. His praying effigy from the late fourteenth century lies in the church and this date seems to show seniority for the haunting.

Folklorists Gutch and Peacock tell of another interesting haunting in Ravendale.[13] They say that in the winter time, a headless man has been seen leaving the ruins of a little church, then walking down the valley. If one were to keep watching, he later returns seemingly happy, with his head under his arm! Whether the state of his mood is ascertained from his gait or the decapitated, smiling head is unclear, but he continues on, resting on a wall where he then utters loud cries of joy. They even say on a certain occasion, a man saw the spectre and actually held the gate open for him, which he passed through, without further ado.

One cannot write about ghosts in Lincolnshire without mentioning Lincoln Cathedral. Such a spectacular building with so much history is bound to collect a few wandering spirits. There have been reports of a ghostly procession of praying monks haunting the Cloisters. The figure of a monk is seen on the steps of the cathedral, and then turns and wanders back inside, sometimes with a chain hanging from his neck. Sightings of a spectre falling from the spire, as he may have done in life, have been recorded, and an immovable bloodstain is said to remain on the floor where a stained glass window master fell to his death after jumping from the gallery.

Perhaps the most well-known haunting is that of Robert Bloet (1094-1123). He was the second Bishop of Lincoln Cathedral and his ghostly horn is said to be heard echoing around the walls. He was not a popular man and there is a legend that he was cursed by Roger the Hermit, a monk from St Albans. This monk had given refuge to a girl, Christina of Markyate, who had run away

The popularly haunted Lincoln Cathedral.

from her husband seeking a life of celibacy. Bloet thought it improper for the girl and the Hermit to live together, saying, 'Bold and insolent...your cowl alone sustains you.'

Roger is said to have made a reply indicating that Bloet would meet an unhappy end and would pray for one in such a cowl but it would be too late. Bloet did meet an unhappy end, being struck down with apoplexy and dying rather swiftly while out riding with the king.

Codd says that the church keepers at the cathedral were forced to perform an exorcism of sorts after his death to eradicate the spirit of Bloet, which had been roaming the building and causing unpleasantness. Even though his spirit has not been seen recently, the horn can, apparently, still be heard on occasion.

The St Peter and St Paul Church at Caistor is also thought to be haunted by a musical religious figure. The ghost of a monk has been reputed to play the organ in the church at night. One vicar, in 1967, tried to quell gossip by placing a cassette player in the church to try and record the sounds, or at least prove there were no sounds to record. He then locked and sealed the building, but when he played the tape back the next day, not only was there organ music to be heard but the sound of footsteps walking through the church, plus strange banging noises too.

As well as old churches and cathedrals, ghosts tend to haunt places that were poignant to them in life. There are many railway hauntings in Lincolnshire, either due to terrible train crashes or workmen who were killed on the lines.

Polly Howat[14] talks of countless Fenland hauntings in her book, many that cross the border into Cambridgeshire or Norfolk, but in one she relays the story of a young boy who saw a ghost at Skegness railway station. It was 1978 and the boy, Mark, was doing some school work in an empty train at platform 6. He was a regular visitor, with family in the railway industry, so the staff knew him and allowed him to sit in the empty cars when he wanted. On this particular Sunday his train was the Shrewsbury excursion train, not due to leave for three hours and none were due to arrive for two. There were no other passengers in the station and the gates were locked from the departure side.

It was with the utmost surprise then, that when Mark rose from his seat he came face to face with an old lady standing in the same coach as he. She was apparently wearing a very old-fashioned purple dress and had a quizzical expression on her face. Knowing all the train timetables, he asked her where she was going, but she didn't reply and a second later she vanished. He exited the train, checking the platform but she was nowhere to be seen and the gates were still locked. He would have been a brave boy indeed to go back and continue with his homework!

Codd also lists a number of railway hauntings on his website.[15] He says that even though it has been closed up and abandoned for years, the signal box at Claxby is said to give out signals to Market Rasen. At Elsham there was a signalman who would hear strange, unexplained noises in the small hours.

The supposedly haunted St Peter and St Paul Church, Caistor.

Platform 6, seen here behind the statue of a friendly traveller at Skegness railway station.

Early one day he heard a bicycle pull up and stop outside the box, but when he opened the door no-one was to be seen. At Elsham Ancholme Bridge a steam locomotive is said to appear, just where several people had been killed in a fatal accident in the 1920s. At Holten-Le-Moor the gate-locking lever in the signal box is reported to ease itself out of the frame for no apparent reason.

It is not just railways – there seem to be a plethora of haunted roads in Lincolnshire, which is no surprise given the number of accident black spots in the county. There was a very interesting *Richard and Judy* show in 1998 when their special guest was the Reverend Fanthorpe from Fortean TV. A man, Kevin Whelan, rang in clearly very shaken about an experience he had just had driving along the A15. Up ahead, just before the left turn to Ruskington, he saw some white lights. Before this incident he never believed in ghosts or the supernatural and was the first to look for a reasonable explanation, so he did not give the lights much thought, believing them to be headlights. As he drew near, however, a face suddenly appeared on the windscreen of the driver's side, with its left hand held up. He described it as having dark hair with olive-grey skin and a pitted face, giving the whole image the semblance of a photographic negative. Kevin was understandably terrified and did well to keep the car on the road. He says the figure must have stayed with him for nearly a full minute before moving down the side of the car and fading away.

After doing some research, Kevin found out that there had been a terrible motorcycle accident there in the last eighteen months, where the rider had died after losing both his legs. He wondered if it had been a warning to slow down, as he had been slightly over the speed limit.

In the same show, two other callers rang in to say they had experienced the same thing in that exact spot. The next show carried on the story, as apparently up to sixty more people had rung in with similar accounts of that same place. Some of the accounts went back ten or fifteen years, so the recent motorcycle accident was not the cause. A follow-up investigation of the area discovered a hermit used to live there and had been run over by an army lorry during the Second World War. Also, in the past highwaymen would hold up stagecoaches in this spot. So perhaps the raised hand could be seen as a cry for help, a warning or a hold-up, but Richard seemed to think it had more sinister connections, as every encounter caused a feeling of fear.

Another reportedly haunted road is the A16, near Walmsgate. Starting in the 1950s, motorists were purportedly witnessing a green glowing mist arising out of an old sandpit and then drifting across the road. Sometimes the mist took the shape of a man before it disappeared into fields on the side of the road. The area became known as Green Man Pit as the sightings became more regular.

A ghost haunted a lane in Boston, but not because of a traffic accident. The *Lincolnshire Life* magazine from 1998 retells the story that was current in 1912 about a miller lad and a baker boy who became friends in Boston.[16] They both had cruel, hard masters and after work they would often meet up and talk about running away overseas together. One day, the miller boy was late to work and his master punished him by throwing him in the marketplace stocks, as an example to all his other workers. People in the busy marketplace jeered at him and threw rotten fruit and small stones at him, but his baker friend was in the crowd and heard his cry. He went to see him and gave him a small loaf of bread as some comfort. The miller boy was very grateful. However, the baker found out and punished the baker lad for stealing his bread. He had him hanged on a gibbet on the crossroads. When the miller boy was eventually freed, he heard about his poor friend's demise and as a sign of their friendship, he ran away to sea as they had both dreamt about. The next spring, a robin built a nest in the jaw of the hanging baker boy's body and began to sing. Straight away people recognised the whistle as that of the baker boy, who used to always whistle while he worked. Rumour spread that he had returned to haunt the baker for the rest of his days, and the baker became so afraid that he dared not pass by the gibbet anymore. It is said that day and night the baker could not get the sound of the bird's whistle out of his head and he eventually lost his mind completely, and consequently all his business too. Belief in Boston is that Gibbet Lane is named after the memory of the baker boy, although his spirit rests in peace now he has found justice.

A much older 'ghost road' story is told by folklorists Gutch and Peacock, concerning Orgarth Hill, near Louth. The haunting was notified in the 1860s and the sighting was that of a man riding on a shaggy horse, which was said to suddenly appear out of thin air and ride alongside people until they were rightly terrified: 'Usually it appeared to people riding or driving, who did not notice the horse and its rider, until they looked to see what had terrified their horses which stood trembling with fear until they bolted down the hill.'[17]

Of course, stories of phantom coach and horses are a familiar tale all around Britain, and Lincolnshire is no exception. In 1985 a lady was driving along the A169 towards Grimsby at dawn. She saw a horse-drawn cart in front of her with no lights and thought she ought to tell the driver. She overtook him but when she looked back in her mirror the cart was no longer there. There had been no turnings they could have taken; they had simply disappeared. Then there is the phantom coach at Ostlers Lane, Maidenwell, whose driver has his severed head on the seat beside him!

Codd tells of a phantom coach and four which pulls into the grounds of Cadeby Hall, near Ludborough and up the driveway – an 'ominous vision [that] was a sign that someone in the family was going to pass away the following day'. The vision apparently appeared only in the evening and then slowly faded from view. He links this apparition to the curse a mother made on Cadeby Hall when her son went missing in the grounds. A child's skeleton was found years later in a hollow tree.

Could this death and curse be linked to that of poor George Nelson, a sixteen-year-old boy who, in 1885, was thrown from his horse and killed close by on Barton Street? Could he be the ghost that a phantom horse reputedly throws into a ditch along this street? There is an engraved stone along the A18 to commemorate his death.

Cadeby Hall, near Ludborough. A private residence, but with a public footpath passing close by.

Stone to commemorate sixteen-year-old George Nelson, who was killed on this spot in 1885. It can be seen by the side of the road along the A18 near Ludborough.

Along a road at Digby Fen there used to be glowing lights seen in the 1900s. The belief was that these belonged to a coach that was accidentally driven into a bog and vanished without a trace. A phantom horseman has also said to have been heard laughing along the road just before Scawby. He apparently got the blame when a local man drowned in a lake that used to be there.

At Girsby, a huge ball of fire used to be seen screaming across the road where the body of a pageboy from Girsby Hall was found, skinned alive. It was supposedly his punishment for betraying some robbers who forced him to help them gain access to the hall to steal its goods. However, another version of this story[18] runs that Billy Hooker was the unfortunate post boy, who had been sent on an errand to collect a parcel of money for his employer. Some robbers apparently got word of this and ambushed him on his return. They demanded the money but Billy refused, so the robbers dragged the poor lad down the hill to what became known as Billy's Hole, where they skinned him alive, draping his skin on the hedge to dry. They ran off with the money, but when they had skinned Billy, they had left the palms of his hands intact and legend has it that this skin grew and grew, eventually re-covering the boy's body in skin once more. The hedge never recovered, however; it has never been able to grow in the place where Billy's skin was draped.

The *Lincolnshire Life* magazine reiterates another interesting ghost story involving burning.[19] It is set in the eleventh century at Monksfield Farm in the Fens. It is said a monastic community lived there, but one night there was a terrible fire and the dormitory was burnt down. Every member of the community died in the fire and every year since, on the anniversary of this tragic event, the ghostly figure of a monk has apparently been seen hurrying across the farmyard with his clothes flaming. It seems that all the locals knew of this ghostly spectre and were very wary of it, but a man called Wellam took the farm over in the nineteenth century and scoffed at the superstition. The tradition had always been to stack the hay in the field but Wellam told the foreman, Glens, he wanted it stacked in the yard from now on. Glens warned him that it would all be burnt, as that was the path along which the flaming monk ran but Wellam didn't believe the story and insisted. He even bet the foreman £5 that the hay would not be burnt. The anniversary came and went and in the morning Wellam found all the hay in the yard had been burnt to a crisp. At first he suspected Glens, thinking he was after his £5, but when he saw how terrified the man was he soon lost his suspicion. The next year he insisted the hay be stacked there again, and he said this time he would keep watch on the anniversary and stop anyone up to mischief, even the blazing monk. However, the next morning the farm workers found his burned and charred body in the yard. No-one ever knew what he had seen.

Lincolnshire has always been a very important centre of military aviation in this country, especially during the First and Second World Wars. In the First World War, there were thirty-seven military aerodromes and Lincolnshire was also the major centre of aircraft production. There were around one hundred RAF stations in Lincolnshire and one can only imagine the numbers of men involved in those operations. The war was a terrifying time for everyone but that fear must have been greatly increased when flying over enemy territory and having to negotiate enemy fire in the air. Of course, there were many casualties and thus many hauntings have been reported, from phantom sounds of squadrons still flying to people talking to airmen who then simply disappeared from sight. Bruce Barrymore Halpenny has written a series of books entitled *Ghost Stations* and he describes numerous experiences and incidents connected with the ghosts of Lincolnshire's RAF.

The Dambusters is perhaps one of the most well-known squadrons in the Second World War, and it was formed at RAF Scampton in 1943 for the specific task of attacking three major dams in Germany. The original commander of this squadron, 617, was Guy Gibson. Guy owned a black labrador retriever who became the mascot of the squadron. Unfortunately, later that year the dog was hit by a car and died on the exact day the squadron launched for the attack on the dams. He was buried at RAF Scampton at midnight, outside the window of Guy's office, as requested by Gibson, and the ghost of the dog is said to haunt the station still. There are stories of a black labrador appearing to guide people who are in trouble, then just disappearing. There have been numerous sightings and his story has become something of a legend. The site of his grave can still be seen and is included in the fascinating and thorough tours of the base, which can be booked by prior arrangement. Also famous as the home of the Red Arrows, the RAF aerobatic team, a tour of RAF Scampton is a must if you are in the area.

The Dambusters Memorial, Royal Square, Woodhall Spa. Another strange incident tells of a black labrador dog appearing and refusing to move when St Hugh's School Choir were posing there for a picture. Still seen in the photograph today, the dog disappeared soon after and no one in the village or surrounding area knew whose dog it was or where it had gone.

The grave of Guy Gibson's black labrador dog, whose death was treated as suspicious as it occurred the night squadron 617 were to set out for the Dambusters raid. One theory was that he was murdered, to make the men think their mission would be jinxed. Guy Gibson's office is the top-right window. Flowers and dog biscuits are placed on his grave every year on the anniversary of this date, and the biscuits are said to have always disappeared by morning!

A stained-glass window in the museum on the RAF Scampton air base, depicting Guy and his dog.

The Red Arrows at home in their hanger at the RAF base at Scampton.

The Black Bull Inn in Welton was apparently a regular pub for Guy and his squadron, and since their deaths it is said the premises are haunted. The landlord allegedly made some tape recordings of inexplicable noises – doors opening and closing and the sound of footsteps walking slowly up to the restaurant, even though no-one was there.

RAF Scampton has a few other ghosts to keep the dog company. A pilot in a life jacket has apparently been seen in the control tower at the airbase and voices have been heard talking in the crew room, even when it was empty. There is also the report of one pilot greeting Lieutenant Salter as he entered the officer's mess, during the First World War. The officer acknowledged him and carried on his way, and it was only later the pilot discovered Salter had died that day in an air crash many miles away and could not have been in the mess at all. A Roman soldier is also said to have been seen walking across the runway.

At the former RAF base at Metheringham, the ghost of a young woman, Catherine Bystock, is said to appear. In life she was a member of the Women's Auxiliary Air Force and engaged to be married to a flight sergeant. She was only nineteen when she was involved in an accident whist riding pillion on his motorbike on the bomber base and was killed. Reports have varied; some say they have seen a girl in a RAF uniform flagging cars down and asking for help for her injured fiancé. However, no fiancé was ever found upon investigation, and when the motorists looked around the girl had vanished too – in some cases leaving behind a scent of lavender.

There are many more hauntings, ghosts, strange sightings and inexplicable occurrences in Lincolnshire's history – too many to mention them all here, but this is a very interesting subject to research if ghosts rattle your chain.

# 6

# WITCHCRAFT AND CUNNING

Witches are not merely mythical crones on broomsticks who fly with their cats at Halloween. They were once imagined to be a major problem in society. The country was apparently overrun with them and like vermin, they were pursued and exterminated. But who were these infamous witches and where did they come from?

Unfortunately, they were usually normal women who became scapegoats during an era of ignorance and superstition, as illustrated in this chapter.

The European witch trials of the Middle Ages is not a period of history we should lightly forget. Present scholars estimate that the number of people who were executed ranges between 40,000 and 100,000, one source suggesting that more than 2,400 of these were Lincolnshire women. There is evidence that as early as 1417, a witch was tried in Sleaford for using divination to trace a thief.

Witchcraft and sorcery are age-old practices, spreading back to when our race was young. One example of this is the *Code of Hammurabi*, which is an ancient law-code not dissimilar to the Ten Commandments. This document, from Babylon, has been dated to 1790 BC, with 282 laws existing on clay tablets. It seems that the first two laws concern witchcraft, with frighteningly familiar – if perhaps slightly fairer – punishments:

> 1. If a man has accused another of laying a death spell upon him, but has not proved it, he shall be put to death.

> 2. If a man has accused another of laying a spell upon him, but has not proved it, the accused shall go to the sacred river, he shall plunge into the sacred river, and if the sacred river shall conquer him, he that accused him shall take possession of

his house. If the sacred river shall show his innocence and he is saved, his accuser shall be put to death.

The book *Malleus Maleficarum* (which translates as *The Hammer of Witches*), subtitled *Which Destroyeth Witches and their Heresy like a Most Powerful Spear*, was written in fifteenth-century Germany and became one of the powerful forces behind the terrible witch hunts that followed.

In the present day we use the term 'witch hunt' to refer to any situation in which someone is persecuted without any concrete evidence – guilty unless proved innocent. Unfortunately, many of the witch trials focused on drawing confessions out of the accused, often through methods of torture or trickery. The witch hunts and trials of the past were spurred on by fear, propaganda, ignorance and misunderstandings.

In many cases, women accused of being witches were healers or those with knowledge of herbal remedies. Alternatively, they may have had a squint in their eye, or a hunched back. They may have angered a neighbour or aroused suspicion by displaying unusual habits or keeping pets. Midwives were common targets, because if they could bring life into the world they might decide to take it away.

As the persecutions increased, more methods of torture for extracting confessions were developed. One such technique was the use of large boots of leather or metal into which boiling water was poured, or sometimes wedges were hammered up the length of the boot into the wearer's legs. Thumbscrews or *turcas* were used to tear off fingernails. Red-hot pincers, crushing, stoning, and the cutting out of the tongue were punishments often employed, together with sleep/light/warmth deprivation and torment with pins. The Witch Finder General's favourite, the swimming test, was amongst the tortures endured. Whilst bound, the accused were lowered into water where, if they sank and drowned they were innocent, but if they floated they would be tried as witches. A physician serving in a witch prison is said to have talked about women who were driven half mad by such techniques:

> ...by frequent torture...kept in prolonged squalor and darkness of their dungeons...and constantly dragged out to undergo atrocious torment until they would gladly exchange at any moment this most bitter existence for death, [they] are willing to confess whatever crimes are suggested to them rather than to be thrust back into their hideous dungeon amid ever recurring torture.'[1]

It is hardly surprising that so many confessions were forthcoming!

The Scottish Forfar Witch Hunts of the 1600s and the Pendle Witch Trials in 1612 are two of the most famous cases in the UK. Lincolnshire, which boasted its very own Witch Finder General, had a case almost as infamous as these; the Witches of Belvoir.

The Earl and Countess of Rutland, who resided at Belvoir Castle near Grantham, employed as servants, in 1618, Joan Flower and her daughters

Belvoir Castle, near Grantham; open to the public.

Margaret and Philippa. Apparently, the countess became dissatisfied with the family, claiming Margaret was pilfering items from the castle, Philippa was conducting lewd activities with her lover and Joan, the mother, was an ungodly and spiteful woman whom she no longer wished to employ. The three were not dismissed immediately but Margaret, who was the only one residing at the castle, was sent home. It seems that it was this action that moved Joan Flower to exact revenge, in the form of cursing the countess' eldest son, Henry. Henry became sick and died shortly afterwards, whilst his younger brother Francis also became ill. Katherine, his half-sister, suffered sudden fits and this 'overwhelming evidence' resulted in the arrest of Joan Flower and her daughters, who were taken to Lincoln Prison.

Joan proclaimed her innocence, demanding the opportunity to prove her case. She allegedly asked for bread and butter, announcing that if she was guilty of witchcraft then she would choke on the bread. The story goes that at the first bite Joan did choke, dying shortly afterwards. This was judged as proof that she had been practising witchcraft against the earl and countess and their family, so the two daughters had no choice but to 'confess'.

They disclosed that Joan had acquired one of Henry's gloves, dipped it in boiling water, stuck pins in it and rubbed it on her familiar, Rutterkin the cat. She then went on to boil the gloves, along with some bed feathers of the earl and countess, in blood and water, attempting to render the couple barren.

A familiar was the special pet of a witch, which was thought to actually be an imp or demon that took on the form of an animal and aided the witch in her Devil worship. These creatures were said to survive by sucking parts of the witch.

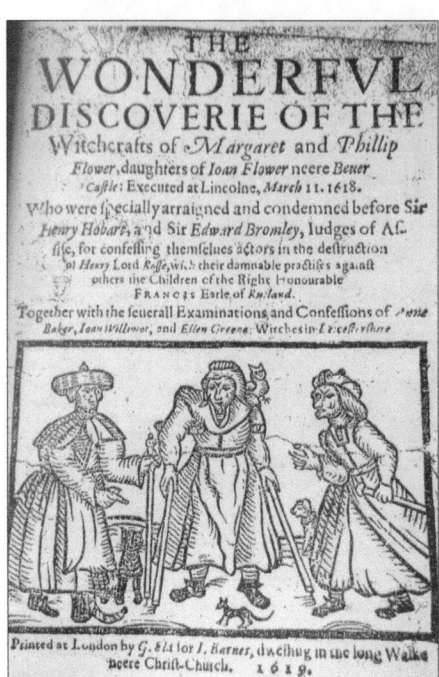

The title page of the first edition of the *Belvoir Pamphlet*, 1619, accusing Joan Flower and her daughters of witchcraft.

A pamphlet concerning these events, named 'The Wonderful Discovery of the Witchcrafts of Margaret and Phillippa Flower, daughters of Joan Flower neere Bever Castle: executed at Lincolne, March 11th 1618' was compiled by one John Barns and details extracts of their confessions. The following is an example, concerning Margaret Flower:

> She saith and confesseth, that about four or five years since, her mother sent her for the right hand glove of Henry, Lord Roos, afterward that her mother bade her go again into the castle of Belvoir and bring down the gloves and some other things and she asked 'What to do?' Her mother replied 'To harm my Lord Roos.' Whereupon she brought down a glove, and delivered the same to her mother, who stroked Rutterkin her cat with it, after it was dipt in hot water, and so prickted it often, after which Henry, Lord Roos fell sick within a week, and was much tormented with the same.

The girls also confessed to experiencing demonic visions and owning familiars of their own, which they allowed to suck at their bodies, then they went on to betray the names of three other women they claimed were also involved.

Anne Baker of Bottesford, Ellen Greene of Stathorne and Joan Willimot of Goodby were duly arrested and eventually made to confess. All three made admissions to consorting with familiars of their own, in the form of a kitten, a mole and a white dog. Ellen Green testified:

Joan Willimott called two spirits, one in the likeness of a kitten, and the other of a moldiwarp (a mole): the first, said Willimott was called Pusse, and Hisse, [sic] and they presently came ot [sic] her, and she departing [sic] and they leapt upon her shoulder, and the kitten sucked under her right ear on her neck, and the mole on the left side in the like place. After they had sucked her she sent the kitten to a baker of that town (i.e. Goadby) whose name she remembers not, who had called her a witch and had stricken her, and had her said spirit go and bewitch hime to death: the mole she then had go to Anne Dawse of the same town and bewitch her to death, because she called this examinate witch, whore, Jade etc, and within one fortnight after they both died.

The women also confessed to having visions, consorting with fairies and uttering curses against people. John Barnes' pamphlet states that Anne Baker was accused of murder by witchcraft:

Being charged that she bewitched Elizabeth Hough, the wife of William Hough to death, for that she angered her in giving her almes of her second bread [i.e. stale]: confesseth that she was angry with her and she might have given her of better bread for she had gone too often on her errands.

He also states that between 1615 and 1618, there were up to eighteen people who were believed to have been injured or killed by witchcraft in the Vale of Belvoir. This again highlights how a crowd can be easily incited by gossip and superstition.

Even though the Flower daughters had already been executed when Francis, the Rutland's youngest son, died in 1620, it was believed by all to be a result of the curses they had inflicted upon him. When the earl died, an inscription was placed at St Mary's Church in Bottesford. This can still be seen there today:

In 1608 he married ye lady Cecilia Hungerford...by whom he had two sonnes, both who died in their infancy by wicked practise and sorcerye.

All counties had their own superstitions about how to avoid the evil eye of a witch. Ethel Rudkin explains some of the local Lincolnshire ones:

In the presence of a witch, so that she shall be powerless against you, clench both your fists with the thumb inside and under the fingers.

If you are bewitched take a lock of hair from low down on the nape of your neck, take another lock from your body, and bury these with needles and pins.

If you pluck a straw from the thatch of a witches' house and hold it in your hand, a witch can't harm you.

The tomb of the Earl of Rutland, on the right-hand side within the church of St Mary the Virgin, Bottesford.

A close-up of the inscription above the Earl of Rutland's effigy, explaining how his sons were killed through witchcraft.

OF BRANDENBOVRG, Y: DVKES OF SAXONY & OTHER GER=
=MAINE PRINCES IN Y: COVRT AT BERLIN : IN 1604 HE
WAS MADE KNIGHT OF Y: BATH & MARRIED Y: LADY
FRANCIS BEVILL ONE OF Y: DAVGHT: & COHEIRS OF Y:
HON: KNIGHT S: HENRY KNYVETT, BY WHOM HE HAD
ISSVE, ONE ONLY DAVGHT: Y: MOST VERTVOVS & THRICE
NOBLE PRINCESSE KATHERINE NOW DVTCH: OF BVCKINGH:
IN 1608 . HE MARRIED Y: LADY CECILIA HVNGERF: DAVGHT:
TO Y: HON: KNIGHT S: IOHN TVFTON BY WHOM HE HAD
TWO SONNES, BOTH W: DYED IN THEIR INFANCY BY WICKED
PRACTISE & SORCERYE : IN 1612 . HE WAS MADE LORD
LEIVETENANT OF LINCOLNESH: & AFTER IVSTICE IN EYRE
OF AIL Y: KINGS FORRESTS & CHASES ON Y: NORTH OF
TRENT : IN 1616 . HE WAS MADE KNIGHT OF Y: MOST
NOBLE ORDER OF Y: GARTER : IN Y: YEARE 1616 HE
WAS ONE OF Y: LORDS WHO ATTENDED KING IAMES BY
HIS MA: SPECIALL APPOINTM: IN HIS IOVRNEY INTO SCOTLAN:
IN 1623. HE WAS BY Y: SAME KING IAMES MADE ADMIR:

If you think that anyone who is ailing is in reality bewitched, then fill a bottle with the sufferers' urine and put needles and pins in it and bury it. This will fairly 'tie the witch up', for she won't be able to pass water naturally until that bottle is broken. [2]

This idea of a witch bottle is a very old device, used to deflect evil energies. Traditionally, once filled with the sufferer's urine, hair, or nails, it was then buried under the hearth or in a secret wall space. Another method was to throw the bottle onto a fire, which broke the spell the witch had cast.

In 2003 there was a remarkable find under some old foundations in the small Lincolnshire village of Navenby. A couple doing some renovations on their house dug up a bottle which seemed to contain bits of metal. They had no idea what it was and put it in a cupboard, eventually taking it along to an open evening at the archaeological department at Lincolnshire County Council.

It was immediately recognised as a witch bottle and dated to the 1830s. It had been damaged, but still had its contents; hair, pins and possibly urine. Adam Daubney, the Finds Liaison Officer said it was an amazing discovery, especially as they thought such superstitions had died out by then. He did state that in the more remote rural areas, old traditions do tend to linger for longer. The bottle is being preserved at Lincoln's Museum of Lincolnshire Life.

Gutch and Peacock say that around 1817, 'a great heap of pins and old fashioned tobacco pipe heads' were found on Hardwick Hill, Scotton Common, 'believed to have been put there for magical purposes'.[3] This is further evidence of the beliefs from this era.

There were various other techniques for trying to ward off the curse or evil eye of a witch. Codd relates the account of a witch from Willoughton who had a reputation for cursing. A certain Mrs Smith decided to invite the witch, Betty, round one day, giving her the best seat in the house to sit upon. When Betty sat down, however, she soon jumped up in pain, as Mrs Smith had hidden pins under the cushion so as to draw the witch's blood and thus deny the witch any power over her. Gutch and Peacock relate the same story happening to a poor old lady, Nanny Moody, from Messingham. She too was tricked into sitting on a chair laced with pins and had a very sore behind for a long time afterwards. She had apparently suffered other incidents from her fellow villagers, who believed she was a witch, but whether she was or not was never confirmed.

This idea of drawing a witch's blood was worryingly popular; Codd tells the story of a pig farmer who complained to the local priest that his pig had been overlooked at market. 'Thou and me knaws the party that hes dun it...'[4] he apparently said, declaring that if only he could draw the blood of the witch then all would be well. What a shocking state of affairs that any woman, young or old, could be charged with being a witch, on the flimsiest of evidence and, like Nanny Moody, be persecuted her whole life.

Other remedies to keep a witch at bay included hanging the skin of a toad on top of a post near the house, or hanging mistletoe above the doorway.

The witch bottle found in Navenby, kindly shown to me by the staff of Lincoln's Museum of Lincolnshire Life, where it is housed. (Reproduction of photograph permitted by Lincolnshire County Council: Museum of Lincolnshire Life.)

*Above left* An example of a witch ball, also held by Lincoln's Museum of Lincolnshire Life. These were apparently hung up in windows to deflect the evil eye, and thought possibly to be the forerunner of Christmas bauble decorations. (Reproduction of photograph permitted by Lincolnshire County Council: Museum of Lincolnshire Life.)

*Above right* Examples of 'witch stones', These were stones with a natural hole in them and were thought to have been used as protection against curses.

The practice of bottling some pins, black apple-pips and hair, then putting the sealed bottle on a hot fire until it burst with heat was a common one. When the glass broke the hex was said to be broken. The wicken tree was used as a tool for warding off evil advances, but the bay and elder were also thought to each contain certain properties to keep a witch away. Gutch and Peacock wrote that mountain ash or rowan twigs (wicken) were carried in pockets, as a charm against witches. Apparently, to avoid having one's pig cursed, you should hang a garland of wicken branches around its neck, then it could not possibly be bewitched.

Gutch and Peacock list a few things people used as charms against witches, including hanging the insides of a pigeon over the door of the house or hanging a horseshoe over the stable door. Iron was often thought of as a weapon to deflect the evil eye, hence the widespread use of horseshoes as 'lucky' charms. Pins and nails worked well too, and a cake stuck full of pins was a good counteract. Cowslips were also thought to be a protection against witches. Witch stones, a stone with a natural hole through it, found accidentally, should be hung in the doorway of a house for protection.

Witches were said to 'eyespell' the first money that a labourer was paid on hiring day, but the men could counter this by spitting on the money or placing it in the mouth.[5]

Lincolnshire was better known for its cunning folk, than for its witches. A Cunning Man was more often seen as a healer, although there was always the fear that he could harm as well. They were more popular than was first thought, although their numbers dwindled considerably during the witch hunts. Charles Kingsley uses this common knowledge of Cunning Men or Wise Women in his novel, when Torfrida asks her nurse to use a charm to discover the mark under her admirer's beard. He also highlights the common belief that witches haunted the Lincolnshire Fens, when Torfrida replies, 'Well, if it keeps off my charm it will keep off others – that is one comfort; and one knows not what fairies, or witches, or evil creatures, he may meet with in the forests and the Fens.'

John Parkins was a well-known Cunning Man who plied his trade in Little Gonerby. He apparently built up quite a business for his charms and protections, calling his establishment The Temple of Wisdom. It is thought that he was an apprentice of the famous Francis Barrett, who tried to revive interest in magical activities after the hunts. As well as protection against witchcraft, Cunning Folk could be fortune tellers, healers and dealers in love potions; some were even said to locate buried treasure.

Wise Men and Women were often called upon by villagers to help them with some problem or other, when the situations arose. Often they were approached by people who believed they were suffering from the curse of bad witchcraft.

Gutch and Peacock illustrate this with a story from Yaddlethorpe about an old man, Thomas K, who was shunned by the entire village, as they suspected him of having the evil eye.[6] Among his crimes were causing rheumatism, cattle to die and pigs not to fatten. His neighbour decided to do something about Thomas K when he found his show horses dead the morning of Lincoln Fair. He visited a Wise Man, who told him to cut out the heart of one of the horses, stick pins into it and boil it. Whilst he was doing this he should expect Thomas K to come knocking at his door, but under no circumstances was he to let him in. The neighbour did all this and apparently Thomas K did come knocking, as predicted, and tried every means possible to enter the house. It was securely locked, however, and the result was that Thomas K became very badly scalded, so much so that he could not work for months.

Another incident is mentioned regarding a lady from the Covenham area, who had been bedridden with a sickness for some length of time. She spread word that she was going to call for the Louth wizard to visit her and aid her recovery. It is said that the very same day she declared her intentions, she was suddenly cured and able to leave her bed. The thinking was that she had been under the influence of some evil eye and that they had lifted the curse, fearing the potential actions of the Wise Man of Louth.

The wizard of Lincoln, known as Wosdel, was called upon one time by a farmer who had been robbed. Wosdel visited, in the form of a blackbird, and showed the farmer the two farm workers who had stolen from him. The men were arrested and the money was eventually found hidden at one of their homes.

Another belief was that the seventh child in a family, male or female, was sure to be 'wise'. Wise Men/Women were thought of as white witches, who used their powers for good, not evil. They possessed a great deal of knowledge and could tell people's fortunes. They were able to look into a person's heart and read their secrets so were respected by all.

Legend states that gatherings or conventions of witch people in Lincolnshire would occur each mid-summer night and some say the burial mound at Revesby was one such meeting place. Others say this was the site of Devil worship, where witches would arrive on broomsticks with stolen un-baptised babies, ready to curse communities with famine and plagues and to dance with the Devil. In 1926, Christopher Marlowe wrote about a visit he made to Lincolnshire and specifically this burial mound. He described bizarre activities going on at the mound – 300 half-naked witches shrieking, dancing, feasting and drinking. He told of a travelling captain who unwittingly stumbled across this company and was badly abused by the witches.

There is a church in Skidbrooke, St Botolph's, which has a reputation for being a centre of black magic and witchcraft, even today. The church itself has not been used for services for over thirty years, but ghosts and Satanists are said to frequent it.

Halloween was an occasion when people were eager to stay indoors, as it was known to be the night of witches and black magic. Katherine Briggs retells a story about witches on Halloween, taken from Barrett's *More Tales from the Fens*. The story teller narrates a tale from his childhood, about an occasion when he stayed at his auntie's one Halloween night. It was the custom this night to place willow twigs around the house, as witches would not cross them and his uncle also apparently killed a black hen, taking two wing feathers to hang on the dog's

St Botolph's Church, Skidbrooke. A beautiful building in a peaceful, rural location. A public footpath leads from the road where there is a sign for 'Historic Church'.

The inside of the church at Skidbrooke – it is completely empty inside, although from the outside it looks like any other church in use. It is fairly large with some beautiful stonework inside.

collar, then tying the hen on the chicken house door. Witches always kept away from black chicken feathers. This was the night that all the witches were supposed to be out in the Fens, meeting up and cursing and placing spells on the people and animals that they came across.

Other precautions included burning oak logs on the fire, as witches could apparently smell peat burning from miles away. Some food was placed on the doorstep to appease any passing witches and thus avoid a curse from them. Before midnight, Barrett was told it was the custom for the oldest man and the youngest boy in the house to go out and do the rounds on the farm, checking on everything. Poor Barrett, who was the youngest lad, was probably terrified with all the talk of witches and curses round the fire!

The two of them trudged outside with a lantern and he said the animals were very restless, as they knew what was out there in the dark. As they walked to the orchard, an owl swooped down at them and the uncle struck out at it with a thick stick, knocking it to the ground. In his opinion he had just slain a witch in flight. They listened in at the beehive and heard a lot of noise going on inside. The uncle bent to it and whispered in, 'Well done, my old beauties. I got one just now and, by the sound of it, you've got another; push her outside when you've done with her.'[7]

Back inside, the others were told of the shenanigans outside and the aunt was nervous of witches coming down the chimney and cursing them before morning. Wanting to discourage any witches coming down, she threw a handful of sulphur onto the fire, making the flames roar bright blue and yellow. The uncle, wanting to go one better, threw a handful of gunpowder he had in the cupboard into the flames. A huge bang shook the house and soot flew everywhere. When the smoke cleared, however, the aunt found herself nursing a dead magpie upon her lap. Another witch down!

After some refreshments, the two males had to do the rounds outside once more and when they got to the beehive, to the boy's astonishment, a dead mouse – still warm – lay on the flight board. The three dead animals were all burnt on the fire and everyone was content that no witches would bother them that night.

It was a very common belief that witches could take the shape of different animals; hares, hedgehogs, cats, toads, magpies…even an ox. The certainty that they could shape-shift in this manner was illustrated by many tales across the county and even appeared in superstition. For example, there used to be a conviction in Kirton-in-Lindsey that eggshells should always be fully burnt or broken, so as to stop witches using them as boats to cross the sea. Quite which animal form they took to accomplish this is unclear, but presumably one quite small.

Daniel Codd mentions the tale of a witch from Dorrington, who used to cause mischief in her village and scared all the locals due to her shape-shifting abilities.[8] She was, however, found one day beaten and bloody in her home and the people believed she had been kicked whilst in the shape of a rat.

There are many stories about witches being hurt whilst in the shape of some animal or other, then when they are seen again in their human form they appear

The church at Tetford, where a gypsy was supposedly struck by lightning on the church steps. She is said to be buried in the churchyard.

to have the same wound as the animal. Codd uses a witch from Rowston as an example. She was known to use the appearance of a hare to travel around but was one day shot by a local farmer whilst in this disguise. She managed to reach her home, but soon died, in human form, from a gunshot wound in her side.

Another well-known witch from Tetford met a similar fate, as she strayed from her house disguised also as a hare. She was shot at, escaped, but later as a human she was discovered with a gunshot wound.

Gutch and Peacock tell of a farmer who was having trouble with his pigs, so one day he took a red-hot poker and scored one pig's back with it.[9] Not long after this incident, a woman in the parish apparently died of a sore back.

On another occasion, a man and his son saw a cat walking in front of them, near Kirton Lindsey. The father knew it to be a witch and so threw a rock at it. The next day, the face of the local witch was heavily bandaged and she died soon after.

Johnny O' The Grass was a famous Wise Man who lived near Louth. His powers of shape shifting extended beyond himself to others as well. It is said that one day he was nearing the toll road, near Girsby Hall and was asked to pay a toll for the donkey he was riding. Men went free. Apparently Johnny dismounted and muttered a few words, upon which his donkey turned into a man, and both men walked the toll road free of charge.

One unusual shape shifter is mentioned in the *Lincolnshire Life* magazine.[10] Set in the days when the Roman Empire was marching its way across Britain, the tale tells of a mounted centurion who was leading his men towards Newport when his horse suddenly stopped for no apparent reason. He dismounted, searching for a cause, checking the horse's hooves and the ground around, but all seemed well. While he puzzled over it, he plucked a blade of grass from the ground and absentmindedly began to tie it into knots. He tried everything he could think to get his horse moving again but it would not budge and his men were getting restless behind him. Infuriated, he threw the blade of grass onto the ground but when he looked down he was astounded to see, not a blade of grass, but a witch with her hands and feet knotted behind her back.

Gutch and Peacock mention an old lame man, who was well known in the area around Northorpe for being a wizard.[11] The shape he would take was a large black dog. Unfortunately, whilst in this guise, he had the habit of biting farmers' cattle. One man was said to have seen him doing this and went to shoo him away, only to see the dog transform into the wizard before his very eyes.

Codd mentions another occasion when a witch at Ludford took a particular dislike to one farm worker, Bob. She was often seen as a white hare, but also a cat and it was this cat that he encountered whilst feeding his horses. She so scared the beasts with her hissing and spitting that they were unable to eat and Bob thought this trouble would earn him a dismissal. His boss, however, believed him and allowed him to place some wicken over the stable door. This tree was often used to ward off or deflect witch's curses and it appeared to have worked on this occasion too.

There is a well-known story of the witch who lived in Scamblesby, who was said to attack and curse anyone who disturbed her. One day, three riders passed too closely by her house and out she rushed ready to curse them. She cast a spell on both the first two horses but the third rider was prepared with a branch of wicken. He was thus protected and could carry on his way, unharmed.

Gutch and Peacock relate a tale of a witch from Grasby whose lover married another woman. She was so distraught that she cursed his cattle, resulting in him losing many of them. He decided he must do something to stop her and so armed himself with some branches of wicken. Whilst he was at home one day, a cat walked into his house and, knowing it was the witch in another form, he chased it around the house until it climbed up the chimney. Wanting to hurt her as he had been hurt, he lit a fire in the grate and scorched the cat badly. Needless to say, the witch died soon after from terrible burns.

Katherine Briggs reports an interesting story from around the Saxby area about the ghosts of six sailors who used to be seen after their ship had been wrecked. They were sometimes seen at night, sometimes during the day, and their faces were always turned towards the sea. One day, a lady decided to talk to them and called to the skipper, whom she recognised. When he replied, however, his voice merely boomed, like a thunder clap and so she had to tell him, 'Moderate your speech, for I'm no 'fit to stand it.'[12]

Soon after this, his speech became just as it had been when he was alive and he told the woman that the witch, Madge Coutts, who had some kind of grudge against them, had boarded their ship in order to curse them. They tried to knock her overboard but when they finally succeeded, she dived under and boarded the other side in the shape of a huge black ox. She set her large horns to work on the decking until she splintered the wood and the boat went under. What grudge she held against the men is not clear but she seemed to survive the incident, as eye witnesses apparently remembered seeing her on the day of the wreck, entering her own chimney in the form of a grey cat.

When discussing their curses, Codd describes the story of a witch mentioned by Rudkin, from the Burton-upon-Stather area.[13] Apparently she was rather a nasty witch and if ever anyone were to cross her or even irritate her, she would place a curse upon them. The incident of a farmer who was unable to deliver her some milk is mentioned and the witch in question is said to have cursed his cow, promising that it would turn into a bull. Supposedly this did happen and the bull became feral and dangerous. The beast was eventually put down, after trying to charge people and causing injury to itself and others.

The witch was said to have also cursed another farmer's whole herd, plaguing the cows with illness. The farmer, however, had a plan to reverse the effects. He chopped seven strands of hair from one of the cows and burnt them at midnight. When the cow began to show signs of improvement, he repeated the ceremony for the rest of the herd and thus saved them from the witch's curse.

Another area of interest in Lincolnshire is that of Byard's Leap, Cranwell. The story depicts Old Meg, a malicious crone, who lived in a cave nearby. This witch was said to curse people, eat human flesh, cause crops to fail and storms to flood the land. All the locals feared her and, as Gutch and Peacock tell us, 'The dread of her, which weighed on the whole country-side, was so great that at last no one dared to resist her. It was thought that no weapon could wound her, and every attempt to withstand her spells had failed.'[14]

Eventually, a retired soldier, or a shepherd in some accounts, came forward claiming he could kill Old Meg by driving a sword through her heart. He needed a swift horse and chose the one that reacted the fastest when he dropped a stone in the pond where the horses were drinking. This horse was blind, known locally as Blind Byard, but his reactions were all the quicker for it. Jennifer Westwood suggests this was a lucky coincidence, as none of the seeing horses would be brave enough to go near the witch, after catching one glimpse of her hideousness.[15] She also proposes that the idea of Blind Byard is an old one in folklore, possibly connected to the story of the French hero Renaud de Montauban and his magical horse, Bayard, or is even linked to the early fourteenth-century proverbial saying signifying recklessness. Nevertheless, in the story the champion apparently rode Blind Byard to the witch's cave and called her out. She called back saying she was busy and he'd have to wait, 'I must suckle my cubs, I must buckle my shoes, and then I will give you your supper.'

The horseshoes at Byard's Leap, Cranwell. These four are easily seen in the car park near the garage, but there are four more hidden in the bushes across the way, similarly presented.

Then she crept up behind him and sunk her long nails into the horse's rump. The poor beast leapt 60 feet into the air, with the soldier clinging to his back. The horse bounded off but the soldier managed to regain control near the pond where he first chose him. The witch chased them all the way there but he was ready for her and when she reached them, he managed to thrust his sword right through her heart, whereby she fell into the pond, dead. There was much rejoicing in the villages and from thenceforth the place where Blind Byard landed from his gigantic leap was named after him and commemorated with four posts in the ground, adorned by horseshoes. The horseshoes are still visible today.

Finally, when reflecting on witchcraft of the past in Lincolnshire and elsewhere, one has to take into consideration all the sociological and psychological influences of that particular time to understand why people believed in ideas which we now think to be dangerous ignorance. Widespread superstition can be seen operating in this old Lincolnshire charm, used when the butter did not come as soon as desired:

Churn, butter, dash,
Cow's gone to th' marsh,
Peter stands at th' toll-gate,
Beggin' butter for his cake;
Come, butter, come.

Three white hairs from a black cat's tail, put into the churn, is another means of insuring that butter will come. The most common method, however, is to take a pinch of salt and put one half in the churn and throw the other half into the fire.[16]

# 7

# YELLOWBELLY SAYINGS AND SUPERSTITIONS

Old George from Holton cum Beckering had left his ancient horse and trap outside the local pub whilst he attended to a little fluid business. After an hour or so's sojourn a young lad popped his head round the door and called out 'Hey up, George! That hoss o' yourn's just fallen down dead in the shafts!' George looked flabbergasted, with his pot half-way to his mouth: 'Well dash my buttons,' he said. 'Do you know, Matey, 'e's niver done that afore!'[1]

We are all guilty of it at some time in our lives – whether we look at the red sky in the evening and expect good weather the next day or think it is a good sign if a black cat crosses our path. The folk of Lincolnshire are no different and the county is home to a whole wealth of humorous sayings, family remedies, strange superstitions, traditions, beliefs, rituals, luck and weather lore, with the inhabitants being known by the delightful nickname of Yellowbellies.

Stories linked to nicknames proliferate – whether it be school boys making fun of each other, politicians trying to undermine one another, counties insulting or giving a fond name to another, or even countries nicknaming each other's inhabitants. In Britain we hear of the Tykes of Yorkshire, the Wiltshire Moonrakers, the Black Army of Llantrisant and, of course, the Lincolnshire Yellowbellies. Mystery surrounds this particular nickname, the exact source being highly debated, and there are variant explanations, even amongst the natives, as to exactly why they have adopted this nickname.

One is that there is a yellow-bellied frog that is native to the Lincolnshire Fens, but there is also a special eel which lives in the wetlands, which has a particular shade of yellow along its stomach. Some say the name derives from here. Alternatively, Lincolnshire, well known for its sheep farming, is renowned for its yellow-bellied sheep, which graze in the mustard fields and get their coats a dirty shade of yellow. The term could have originated because the waistcoat of the Lincolnshire Regiment's uniform was yellow and the fastenings, also yellow, were called frogs; a reference to the native Fen frogs perhaps. It was also said that when farm workers were labouring in the sun and stripped off their shirts, that although their backs turned a nice shade of brown their tummies went yellow.

Another theory concerning the colour of the skin stemmed from the fact that ague (a form of malaria) was prevalent in the Fen country and that the medicine, extracted from poppy heads, turned the skin a yellowy colour. Also, it is said that women trading at market stalls had two pockets in their leather aprons, one pocket for the silver coins and one for gold. If they declared they had a 'yellow belly' at the end of the day, it was a sign they had taken plenty of gold. Similarly, it could be that the wealthier farmers would carry gold in a bag around their waists as they travelled to market.

The *Lincolnshire Life* magazine suggests the idea could have come from the Coningsby tradition,[2] whereby men were served a feast of bacon, 'tates', swede, turnip etc, upon an oval-shaped plate with blue edging. Copious amounts of butter adorned the meal and the whole thing was apparently known as 'a Lincolnshire Yellowbelly on a blue-edged plate'. Whether the saying or the meal came first is unclear.

There is the story of a poor lass from Ingham who no-one would marry. In the end, her father was so desperate to be rid of the poor girl that he promised that any man who would take her off his hands would receive enough gold sovereigns as would cover her fat belly! Could this be the origin of the nickname? Some say those Fen slodgers, men who made their livings catching fish and fowl in the wetlands, crept around in the mud so much that it turned their bellies yellow!

Another story in the folk tales of the past tells of a group of ship wreckers from Cleethorpes who one night lured a ship onto the rocks, only to discover the cargo was solely made up of a yellow-coloured flannel material. Unable to sell it on but not wanting it to go to waste, the villagers and townspeople nearby made undergarments from it, thus becoming known as the yellow bellies.

On a more historical note, some believe the term stems from Ye Elloe Bellie, which has its roots in the name of the rural deanery for the Lincoln Diocese, and is also linked to a Saxon Wapentake, or meeting place, in the area. Perhaps the term derived from the old Lincolnshire mail coach drivers in the 1700s, who always wore long yellow waistcoats, distinguishing them from the drivers of other parts of the country. Or was it to do with the yellow colour of the coaches themselves?

The quandary as to the real origin of the phrase is part of the charm of the nickname and thankfully so, as the true meaning may never be discovered.

As well as having an affinity with yellow, Lincolnshire, famous at one time for its woollen cloth and textile industry, was very well known for its Lincoln Green. This is the bright green colour of dyed woollen cloth, through a mixture of using woad – to create a strong indigo – then over dyeing it with weld root, which gives yellow – creating the Robin Hood green we know well.

Britain is saturated with superstitions and old beliefs concerning birth, marriage, wealth, death, animals and even the weather. Before the invention of television, the fireside was the centre of every household. At night, the family would gather round to keep warm and stories, tales and wisdom would be told and re-told, passing down from generation to generation. This is where much of the old folklore and knowledge came from and it is a shame times have changed so much that this sort of tradition is not a priority for families nowadays. It was so important then that, as the *Lincolnshire Life* magazine tells us, people in this county would bury items beneath the hearth when the house was being built to ensure good luck and dispel any bad atmosphere.[3] Even the fire itself was the source of superstitions: smoke going straight up the chimney meant rain was on its way; blue flames were a sign of frost; and soot falling onto the fender indicated a visitor was coming. Apparently throwing bread onto the fire in Lincolnshire was a bad idea as it was seen as feeding the Devil.

There are many superstitions about marriage up and down the country – some of them particular to certain counties, others holding sway the country over. For instance, the colour of the wedding dress is important to all brides, even today. The colour white is the most commonly used and is thought to denote innocence and purity. Green, however, was seen as ill-advised as it was the fairies' colour and would attract their unwanted attention. Yellow was unpopular, dating from the Middle Ages when slaves and bankrupts were dressed in the colour. Some say this may be why the Nazis forced the Jews to wear a yellow Star of David. Blue, however, is a lucky colour, signifying heaven and constancy, showing the wife will be an honest woman and a hard worker; thus the old saying, 'Something old, something new, something borrowed, something blue.'[4]

The day and time of year for a wedding is also shrouded in superstition, with many pithy sayings surviving, such as 'marry in Lent, live to repent'. Another old saying goes, 'Change the name and not the letter, change for worse and not for better.'

One old belief, which nearly all married couples adhere to, even today, is to wear the wedding ring on the fourth finger of the left hand. This is because it was thought that this particular finger had a vein running through it which led straight to the heart.

The confetti ritual in Lincolnshire originated when wheat was thrown, as a symbol of fertility for the newlywed couple. Also there used to be a tradition of the bride wearing a necklace styled in the form of a corn dolly, placed around her neck by her mother on the wedding morning. The groom often wore a small corn dolly in his button hole, attached by his father. This too was used as a symbol of fertility and contentment, the corn dollies being kept by the married couple all their lives. It is said that later, the carrying of carnations was a replacement for the corn dolly.

An old legend from Lincoln stated that the reason the bride would always have bridesmaids was that it was a way of distracting evil spirits – they would see a number of women all dressed alike and would not know which one was the bride and therefore could cause her no mischief. Bridesmaids and other unmarried girls at the wedding would take a crumb of the wedding cake, pass it through the wedding ring and then sleep with the piece under their pillow. They were then said to dream of the man they would marry. There were many rituals and beliefs concerning future partners – relationships and marriage being of much importance, especially to women.

St Mark's Eve (24 April) was said to be the night ladies could divine who they were to marry. They used to visit the Maiden Well at North Kelsey, walking towards it backwards and then circling it three times, still backwards, whilst wishing to see their destined husbands. After the third circling, the girl would kneel and gaze into the spring, where she would supposedly see the face of her lover.

Another superstition stated that on the same day, if they set up their table with supper and left the door open, their future husband would walk through the door and join the meal. However, on the same night, the young men were said to be able to find the face of their future bride in the church window, if they went to the churchyard at midnight. The inevitable question arises; if the gentleman was wondering around in the graveyard, would he be in time for supper at his sweetheart's house? Or perhaps he needed to go to the churchyard to find out which girl's house he was supposed to be visiting!

Alternatively, when eating an apple, the girl could throw the unbroken peel over her left shoulder and when it fell it would fall in the shape initialling the name of her future partner. Similarly, the practice of naming the chestnuts roasting over the fire was an option – the first to crack signalled the boy the girl would marry. Or on the eve of St Thomas (21 December) ladies would take a peeled onion to bed with them and place it under their pillow, with the belief that one would dream of the man they were going to marry. Although somewhat unreliable, some of these practices were viewed more seriously than others.

Legend had it that if the youngest daughter married before her sisters, they should all dance barefoot at her wedding in order to secure themselves husbands of their own. A tumble when going upstairs was a sign that the person would soon be married, and three lamps burning on a table together was a sign of a wedding in the family.

Roy Palmer reiterates one peculiar belief regarding riches. He tells that it was once thought that if a wealthy woman should marry a man with debts, the creditors could not touch her money if she performed the ceremony naked. He says this particular belief was actually carried out by a bride in Gedney, in 1842 – reported in the *The Times* newspaper. It was, however, December and the story states the lady was covered with a sheet.

There is an old Lincolnshire saying, once well understood, whereby a countryman would tell his sweetheart that he would marry her, '...when the bods (birds) hes two taäils'.[5] One can be forgiven for assuming this means the man will never marry the lass – but in actual fact it was an indirect way of telling her he would marry her in the spring, when the swallows arrived.

If you want to know whether your lover is being faithful to you or not, throw an apple pip onto the fire. If it cracks and spits, the partner is faithful, but if it merely withers and burns they are being unfaithful.

Roy Palmer talks of 'riding the stang', which was also known as 'charivari' and practised for over 700 years. It refers to a tradition of the community gathering together if they disapproved of something, such as adultery, a marriage of a widow, the union of a widower to a much younger bride (often referred to as 'as thick as thatch'), or the news that a man was beating his wife. They would choose an area in the village and then commence making a racket with any means possible. They would sing and shout, bang pots and pans and cause noisy, discordant 'rough music' to demonstrate their disapproval. The actual 'riding of the stang' refers to placing the target backwards on a horse and parading them through the streets, surrounded by the noise and people mocking them. Palmer quotes a song that was used in Lincolnshire for a wife beater:

Ran tan tan, the sound of the old tin can.
Mr Timothy Wobblechops has been beating his good woman;
Nather for wop not for why
He up wi' his fist and he blacked her eye,
But if he does it again,
Which I suppose he will,
We'll take him to the beck
And give him a good swill.
If that won't do we'll skin him
And send him to the tanner,
And if they won't tan him well
We'll hang 'im on the nail o' 'ell.
If the nail o' 'ell should happen to crack
We'll put him on the Devil's back.
If the Devil should happen to run
We'll shoot him with a gun.
If the gun should happen to miss
We'll scald him to death with a barrel o' red hot piss.[6]

He states that this system was applied to two men at a village west of Gainsborough, whereby one of the men eventually hanged himself and the other ended up in a madhouse.

Rudkin gives an example of a schoolmaster in Holton-le-Clay who was a very bad-tempered man. He apparently gave one of the school boys a harsh thrashing and then tied him by his thumbs to a washing line, where he left him to hang. The villagers were so outraged that they 'ran-tanned' the schoolmaster for three nights together. With sticks they spent the nights banging and hammering sheets of iron and old kettles outside his house, whilst singing and humiliating him.

Then they burnt a straw effigy of him outside the public house. Certainly a lesson learnt there!

In days gone by when the Church had greater influence in communities than it does in most places today, many Lincolnshire folk were Christian and believed every child must be baptised. This involved placing salt on the tongue of the baby, to drive away the Devil. One of the old superstitions said that a newborn baby's hands should not be washed until after it had been christened, the accumulated dirt being a sign of its future wealth. Some thought the longer the christening robe, the longer the life of the infant, and the sign of a well-made shawl was that it was fine enough to pass through a wedding ring. Another idea stated that the baby should be made to 'sneeze' out the Devil when first born. Some people said that if a child was born with its hands open that it would be a kind and generous person, but if its hands were closed it would prove to be rude and unpleasant.

If church bells were heard ringing the moment a child was born it was believed they would be very lucky – as bells drive away evil spirits, whereas to cut a baby's hair or nails with scissors or a knife was unlucky. The best way was to bite the nails if they were getting too long. If cut before the baby was a year old, some said it was a sign they would grow up to be a thief. If the mother wanted to keep evil away from her baby, an old saying stated that she should never allow her hands to be idle whilst she rocked the cradle.

While everyone had open fireplaces within their homes, the shapes the soot from the fire created were 'read' like tea leaves. The shape of a crescent moon apparently meant a cradle would soon enter the home, whereas a rectangular shape indicated a coffin, and a death.

The *Lincolnshire Life* magazine tells of an old tradition where midwives and nurses wore belt buckles of intricately knotted patterns so as to distract evil spirits who had come for the mother and child at the most vulnerable time – the birth.[7] However, the fancy belts steered their attention away and the mother and baby stayed safe.

Loosening hair would help with a difficult birth, and keeping the 'silly hood' – the membrane covering a baby's head at the time of birth – was thought to bring luck and long life.

The *Lincolnshire Life* magazine tells that the godparents were given the task of taking a piece of cake with them to church for the baby's christening.[8] The first person they met of the opposite sex to the baby was given the cake – and if that person was cross-eyed it was a sign of good fortune. It also states that there used to be a tradition of entering the church via the south/south-west door for the christening, but leaving the north door open. If the baby cried when the water was poured onto its head, that was a sign that the Devil had left the child's soul and run back to hell through the open north door.

If your daughter was born with hair that grew into a peak on her forehead the belief stated that she would never marry, or would have a very short marriage, hence the term 'widow's peak'.

A commonly held belief was that if a woman were to sit on the same chair where a pregnant woman had been seated, she would be the next to become pregnant, but in Lincolnshire this idea extended to sitting on the bed whilst visiting a new mother. The belief in Navenby was that if a young woman was to sow parsley seeds then she would have a child. At one time the new mother was offered an egg from visitors, both for nourishment and also as a symbol of fertility – may she go on to have many more children. If this happened during the harvest time, the mother would be offered a small bunch of wheat.

Ever wondered why baby girls are dressed in pink and boys in blue? One theory suggests that pink dye was cheaper to produce and as boys were once thought to be more valuable than girls they had the superior dye. Charming!

Katherine Briggs relates an interesting story of superstition about two men travelling through Lincolnshire.[9] They were on foot and getting weary so they lay down by the roadside to rest awhile. One of the men fell asleep and while he napped, the other man saw a bee buzzing around then settle on a nearby wall and crawl into a small hole. The watching traveller idly put the end of his staff into the hole and blocked the bee's exit.

He soon wished to carry on their journey and so decided to wake his partner, but his friend was so fast asleep that he would not be roused. Baffled, the man removed his stick from the wall, noticing the bee fly directly out; he watched it fly into the slumbering man's ear. The man instantly woke up and said he had had a very deep sleep, but a very odd dream. He remarked that he had dreamt his companion had shut him up in a dark cave and he could not wake up until he was let out. After hearing this, the man who had stayed awake was convinced that his friend's soul was in the bee!

Bees, it seems, held a role of relative importance in old Lincolnshire life. There was a belief that they had to be informed when there was a death in the family, otherwise the bees would search relentlessly for the deceased and when unable to find them would die themselves. They also took part in the mourning process, with a piece of black cloth being draped over the hive. It is said they should be offered some of the funeral wine and informed who the new master of the house would be, or they would leave their hive.

Gutch and Peacock relate an incident witnessed in a house at Stallingborough in the 1800s. It took place a few days after the death of the cottager, when a visitor asked the widow if she had informed the bees of the master's demise. When hearing this had not been done, she took some cake and went out into the garden, offering the cake to the hive and chanting:

Honey bees! Honey bees! Hear what I say!
Your master, J.A., has passed away.
But his wife now begs you will freely stay,
And still gather honey for many a day.
Bonny bees, bonny bees, hear what I say.[10]

They were also used as an omen for a death in the family, if one were to see a swarm settling on a dead branch of a tree.

Death, like marriage, had many superstitions and rituals attached to it, such as the idea that upon a death, all the goods within a household should be shaken so that the sad news was known by all.

It was said that if a picture fell from the wall above the fire into the hearth it was an omen of a death in the family. A high wind was also a sign of death, specifically the death of a distinguished person and the failure of the crop of ash-keys was said to portend a death in the Royal family. To eat off a plate with another plate beneath it foretold a death.

If a married woman with normally straight hair suddenly found two curls on her temples it was a sign that she would soon become a widow. Ethel Rudkin tells of a lady from Scawby who found two such curls over her temples; she was terrified, knowing what it meant. Within a fortnight her husband was dead.[11]

There are many superstitions concerning death in Lincolnshire attached to candles. It is said the guttering of a candle is a sign of a death, as is the way the wax melts down the side of the candle. A candle should not be allowed to die out, or it is thought to bring death to a sailor out at sea. The death of another family member is prophesied within the year if the candle burning next to a dead body should fall out of its holder.

Gutch and Peacock quote a belief reported in the *Horncastle News* in 1894: 'A strange legend is current in Swineshead that, 'If a corpse lies in a house on Sunday there will be three within the week.'[12] Also, if the passing or funeral bell is tolled in the church by mistake when the bells are being rung, then a death will follow shortly after. Another sign a death will soon occur is having an odd number of people in a funeral procession.

It was thought that if one were to sew on a Sunday then they would prick their finger and die of the wound. Ethel Rudkin tells of the superstition that if someone tried to attract your attention by waving a shovel at you, that you should throw a handful of earth in their direction immediately or else it was an omen you would soon be buried.[13]

It was an age-old belief that a person could not die in a bed which contained pigeon's feathers. With this in mind, on some occasions, if someone was taken suddenly ill and seemed likely to pass away before some particular relative arrived, a small bag of pigeon feathers was placed under the pillow, in order to hold death back.

If you had the misfortune to be bitten by a fox, the belief was that you would die within seven years. And woe betides the person who heard a cock just before midnight. This was a sign of either their own demise or of someone close to them. A pigeon flying into the window of a room where there was a very ill person was seen as a sign that they soon would die. Many superstitions surrounding death were attached to birds – doves, magpies, pigeons, cormorants – and a death bird would often make an appearance at the hour of fatality.

It was customary in Lincolnshire for the window of a dying person to be opened, and then after they had died all the other windows of the house should be opened, with the blinds drawn down.

Belief in the 'dead cart' was rife in Lincolnshire at one time. The legend stated that a horseless cart would travel the streets in the early hours, carrying the dead souls away and that if you were unfortunate enough to hear the wheels of the cart as it passed, or to look out of your window and see it, then it was an omen that either you or someone in the house would die within three days. During the funeral of the deceased, it was customary in some parts of Lincolnshire to leave the door of the house open, so that if the spirit of the dead person wished to return home they would not be shut out.

If one were to accidentally fold their tablecloth carelessly, so that diamond-shaped creases were formed, then this was seen as a sign of death. A lighted fire that had been forgotten about but burnt on late into the evening, even without any new fuel being placed upon it, foretold news of a death. Gutch and Peacock state that it used to be considered very bad luck to take hawthorn blossom indoors, as this was seen as a precursor of death.[14] They also state that it used to be the practice in most Lincolnshire churches to hang a garland from the roof of the church when a young unmarried woman died. If a woman died during childbirth, the custom used to be to throw a white sheet over her coffin and in some parishes she was carried by maidens wearing white hoods.

If a child was dying in the house, three horseshoes were to be placed at the foot of the bed and struck with a wooden mallet, whilst the father chanted:

With this mell I thrice do knock,
One for God, one for Wod and one for Lok.[15]

As the *Lincolnshire Magazine* states, this is a fine example of the overlap between the old pagan beliefs and the new Christian ones – a father hedges his bets and prays to both sides for help. The magazine also states that in days gone by it was the custom for men to carry the coffins of men in the funeral procession, women to carry women and maids to carry maids. Sometimes a bowl was made available at the funeral for friends to leave pins, a long-held belief that this would help keep evil spirits away. Metal was often used to frighten away evil spirits, another example being during sowing season. The horses would be dressed with a metal piece on their head and breast gear to protect their hearts from the evil sprites.

One gentle, old belief, mentioned in *Lincolnshire Life* magazine, was that a man puts his fire into a woman and that when he dies she turns to the hearth fire for comfort.

Daniel Codd recounts a tale connected with the old Lincolnshire superstition about the elder tree. Elder was sacred to Hecate, the ancient Greek Goddess of death and childbirth. There was a belief that the Elder Queen lived in the roots of the elder tree and that if one were to cut the branches without her permission, one would risk blindness, a loss of health, livestock illness or even a death in the family. People would also be expected to appease the Elder Mother with offerings and charms and if they wanted some of the wood from the tree there was a special way to ask the Lady's permission: 'Owd Gal, give me some of thy wood, and Oi will give thee some of moine when Oi graws inter a tree.'[16]

Codd says there is a story of a baby's cradle being made with ill-gotten elder wood and that the poor child had been snatched from under his parent's eyes, never to be seen again. However, if one is caught out in a thunder storm, choose an elder tree to stand under, as legend states lightning will never strike the Elder Mother!

Another strange tree legend has attached itself to a palm tree, thriving unexpectedly near the church porch at Ingoldmells. It supposedly sprouted up of its own accord when the squire's daughter died of a broken heart, when her lover fled abroad after the discovery of their affair.

Mistletoe cut from an oak tree is thought to bring victory in a battle if carried around the tree sun-wise three times, and cows were once encouraged to eat the leaves of mistletoe as it was meant to deflect any curses a witch may have put on the dairy. If one is to bring blackthorn into the house it portends someone will break their arm or leg. Bunches of hazel and willow placed in water upon a windowsill are said to protect against thunder and lightning.

There is a tale surrounding St Mary's Church in Stow, which is supposed to stand on the site of a miracle. Around AD 670, the Northumbrian Queen Etheldreda was fleeing across Lincolnshire to Ely, when she stopped to rest at

The mysterious palm tree growing next to the St Peter and St Paul Church porch in Ingoldmells, Skegness.

# YELLOWBELLY SAYINGS AND SUPERSTITIONS 141

St Mary's Church, also known as Stow Minster, situated on the site of a miracle.

Victorian stained-glass window, high up on the north wall of the chancel, to the left of the alter in Stow Minster, depicting Etheldreda and her staff.

Just outside Stow Minster are some whipping irons dating back to 1789, complete with the maker's stamp mark.

Stow. It was a tremendously hot day and the poor lady had no shade in which to rest, and so had to make do with what she found. Lying on the grass she stuck her staff in the soil beside her and fell asleep but when she awoke, she found that her staff had put forth branches and leaves to protect her from the sun. The staff grew into a huge ash tree and pilgrims travelled far and wide to visit it. Now there is an extremely large church on the spot, one much too big for the small village of Stow, but people call it the 'Mother of Lincoln Cathedral'. There is a stained-glass window left of the altar to illustrate the legend.

Codd also relates the story of a poor post boy who was savagely slain by two highway men.[17] Legend has it that the murder was so horrific that the grass around the lad's grave at Nettleham refused to grow.

Gutch and Peacock mention a legend surrounding a black stone at Crowle.[18] Apparently it was believed that if the stone was removed from the farmyard then all the cattle would die within a year. It was even reputed to have happened to one particular farmer, but the stone was replaced after this incident.

'Were you born in a barn?' This is a common saying for someone who habitually leaves doors open after them, but there is a village in Lincolnshire which has customised the saying to suit a miracle that happened in their area. Bardney was once the home of Tupholme Abbey where King Oswald of Northumbria's remains were taken after he was defeated in battle against

The gravestone under the tree, with no grass growing around it, is found in Nettleham churchyard, to the left-hand side of the church. Tho Gardiner is named as the post boy of Lincoln, 'barbarously murdered by Issac & Tho Hallam Jan 3rd 1732. Aged 19'.

King Penda of Mercia, in AD 675. However, upon arrival, the monks left the king's remains out in the field, as they regarded him as an enemy. Later that day, they were amazed to see the spot where they had left the dead king lit up with a bright beam of light from the heavens. They took the sign as a warning from God to treat everyone equally and not to close their doors to anyone. Thus the saying, 'You must have been born in Bardney!'

It has been said that once, no mice or rats were to be found at Fishtoft. The legend stated that so long as the whip in the hand of the statue of St Guthlac, in the church, was intact, the village would be free from mice and rats. Unfortunately for the residents, the whip is now long gone.

Gutch and Peacock relate a strange old folk belief that if you wanted to know whether a mare was with foal or not, one had to take a mouthful of water and spit it violently into the beast's ear.[19] If she shook her head it was a sign she was with foal whereas if she shook her whole body then she was not.

A white blemish on the thumb nail was said to foretell the arrival of a present. Each finger also held a different omen if the mark appeared on them; friendship, an altercation, romance and an imminent journey.

To scare a poor child who had an inflamed spot or bite on the face, the custom was to tell them that a pig's foot was growing there. Some other sayings to tell children were less frightening; thunder was said to be

The ruins of Bardney Abbey, just across the field from a car parking area; signposted from the village.

Statue of St Guthlac, minus his hand and legendary whip, standing above the west door of the church at Fishtoft.

'elephants falling out of bed' and snow was 'the Old Lady shaking her feather pillows out of her window'.

A well-known Lincolnshire answer to a child's awkward question was, 'How should I knaw, bairn; why does craws pick lambs' eyes oot?' When a child asked why they would not play, the adult answered, 'I've got a bone in my leg.' The question 'Where are you going?' was answered with, 'There and back again to see how far it is.' And the enquiry 'What's that for?' had the reply, 'Just for fancy, to please old Nancy.'

A canny belief among Lincolnshire children was that if they were to see a white horse pass by, then they should spit on the ground and cross their feet over it, then they would shortly receive a present.

Many places in the country have a rhyme about the magpie, but Lincolnshire has its own version:

One, for sorrow; Two, for mirth;
Three, for a wedding; Four, for a birth;
Five, for a fiddler; Six, for a dance;
Seven, for Old England; Eight, for France.[20]

Not far from the centre of Fishtoft, signposted from the village, is a memorial to the Pilgrim Fathers who tried to sail from this area in 1607. The tower of Boston Stump can be clearly seen from this spot.

G. Edward Campion explains that in Lincolnshire there are variations for the meaning of the word 'parson'. As well as a minister of religion, he says it also denotes a black lamb. A superstition commonly believed at one time was that when one saw the first lamb of the season, you should turn over the money you had in your pocket and then you would be bestowed with good luck. This action should also be taken when seeing the first new moon of the year, or when hearing the first cuckoo. If you did not happen to have any money in your pockets it was considered bad luck and you would be short of money all the rest of the year. Superstition around money was important and it was said that to ensure good luck for the day, any tradesman would spit on the first money they receive that morning.

'Parson' also meant a black rabbit and it was apparently considered extremely bad luck to shoot one. Campion says that if a black rabbit was shot, the luck of the shoot would fade away and that the bag at the end of the day would be very small.

A fourth meaning for the word 'parson' was a guide-post and so a lost traveller, for instance, would ask 'What does the parson say?' With typical Lincolnshire humour the signpost was called a parson because it points the way to go, but does not take it.

Luck, good and bad, has always had superstitions attached to it, such as not opening an umbrella indoors, or not walking under ladders. In Lincolnshire it was thought that to place an umbrella on the bed would bring bad luck but to walk into a church with the right foot first would bring good luck. If you moved into a new house or married on a Saturday it was a bad start and another bad luck occurrence would be if two people were to look simultaneously into a mirror or cross knives at the dining table. One should also never place a pair of new boots onto a table. To put the left shoe on first when dressing was considered bad luck, but to throw an old shoe after someone who was starting a new business meant good luck for them. If you saw a pin on the ground it was thought lucky to pick it up but to pick up a flower that had been dropped was bad luck. If you dropped your stick when out walking, someone else must pick it up for you or else bad luck would follow, possibly an argument with someone. This was also considered true when dropping an umbrella, money or a comb. To burn mistletoe, even by accident, was always seen as a bad omen.

Cross yourself when seeing a solitary magpie or bad luck will follow. The swallow, however, was a good omen, especially if it made a nest on your house; this would protect you from being struck by lightning. When making the bed, do not flip the mattress on a Sunday as this would bring bad luck all week long. Four was believed to be a lucky number, but the name Agnes was unlucky, as the bearer would invariably turn mad!

Singing before breakfast was a sure sign that one would cry before night and laughing before praying in the morning, or after praying at night, would also bring misfortune. One should not sweep out a doorway, for fear of sweeping luck away.

It used to be the custom for sellers to give a little of the asking price back to the buyer, for luck. It is said friends should never wash their hands in the same water, unless they first spat into it, otherwise a quarrel was inevitable.

When a cow had recently calved, it used to be customary to make a rich custard pudding with her milk and to give friends a gift of this milk. The rule was, however, that the jug in which the milk had been carried to the friends must be returned unwashed, otherwise misfortune would follow.

Gutch and Peacock told of an old tradition concerning a double nut.[21] If one cracks a nut and it turns out to be double, the common practice was to share the nut with a friend and whilst eating, both were sanctioned to make a wish, but to keep that wish a secret – rather like when blowing the candles out on a birthday cake, or sharing a wishbone with someone. In Lincolnshire it was also the tradition to make a wish when tasting the first strawberries of the year.

They also mention the story of a poor man who was killed on the railway lines near Mumby. When talking about the incident later, a local was heard to have said that it was not a strange event, as the man had been approached by a carrier earlier in the day who wanted to kill a duck for his tea. He asked the deceased to hold the duck while he killed it; this was his fatal mistake. It is mortally unlucky to hold anything whilst it is dying.

Apparently, especially around the Barnoldby-le-Beck area, it was thought to be very bad luck to take your cat with you if you moved house. However, if you had to take it, then the idea was to rub its paws with butter in the new house, or leave it locked in the (cold) oven overnight, and it would then surely stay in the new house.

For brides it was thought very unlucky to tear the veil, as it was a sign the marriage would not last. To forget or to drop something on the way to the church was also a bad omen as it signified looking back instead of forward to a new life with her husband.

When playing cards it was customary for ladies to turn their chairs round three times for good luck during the game. For good fortune during the time of the moon, one should bow or curtsey at the first sight of the new moon, and to avoid bad luck, burning evergreens that were used for Christmas decorations was to be avoided. A flock of sheep was thought to be unlucky if it did not have one black one amongst them.

It was said to be bad luck if, on seeing a dead body, one should leave without touching it. It does not seem to matter if you knew the unfortunate person or not – not touching them would lead to hauntings and nightmares of the departed.

Gutch and Peacock cite a rather unusual belief that the people around Barboldby-le-Beck used to trust: 'Shrews and Hedgehogs are always to be killed, if possible. Vague, unknown powers of mischief are theirs.'[22]

It is not entirely clear why these particular animals were hated, although there are a number of suggestions. It was once believed that witches would transform themselves into hedgehogs to escape or hide from people, and thus hedgehogs were not to be trusted. Also hedgehogs were known for suckling cows in the night and leaving the farmer short of milk, and for sucking eggs, thus being a costly nuisance to the farmer. They were known for stealing apples as well, apparently carrying them on their spines by rolling on them to attach the fruit. There was even a well-known saying when talking to a bad-tempered person: 'You've yer back up today like a peggy otchen goin' a crabbin,' (a 'peggy otchen' being a hedgehog and the 'crabbing' the apples.)

Shrews and hedgehogs were also accused of biting other animals, giving them the same swelling symptoms as an adder bite and thus wasting a poultice for treatment. This hatred obviously came before our roads got so busy and the hedgehog population became threatened. Their species was once much more prolific, so much so that before barbed wire was invented, farmers used to use the skins of hedgehogs on gate-posts to stop the cattle rubbing themselves against it.

Being a huge farming community, the people of Lincolnshire put much stock in what the weather was doing and have many a saying about how it behaves and what that means for them. For instance, duckweed seen rising in a pond was a sign of fine weather. When frogspawn was at the side of a pond it was thought that it signalled a wet summer, and when in the middle of the pond it would be a dry summer. Folk believed that every month had its own weather and that a deviation in that system was not a good sign for crops:

A January Spring
Is no fine thing.

February, for instance, was nicknamed 'February Fill Dyke', as snow was always expected during this month and it was seen as very unusual for there to be none:

> Warm February, bad hay crop.
> Cold February, good hay crop.

Candlemas, an ancient festival marking the midpoint of winter between the shortest day and the Spring Equinox, celebrated on 2 February, was an important time, with its own omens and superstitions:

> If the sun does shine on Candlemas day
> Saddle your horse and go buy hay
> If Candlemas day be fair and bright
> Winter will have another fight
> If Candlemas day be wind and rain
> Winter is gone and won't come again.

However, the weather, it seems, was still fairly unpredictable, as some of the following ditties imply – although perhaps not as unpredictable as what we have now, with the changes that global warming has brought about:

> If in February there is no rain
> 'Tis neither good for hay nor grain.

> Fogs in February mean frosts in May.

> If the first three days of April be foggy
> Rain in June will make lanes boggy.

> If it thunders on All Fool's Day
> It brings good crops of corn and hay.

> A cold wet May
> Brings plenty of corn and hay.

> In November
> If there's enough ice to bear a duck
> All the rest of the year will be slush and muck.

> A light Christmas, a light harvest.
> A green Christmas, a full churchyard.

The oak before the ash
You'll only get a splash.
The ash before the oak
You're bound to get a soak.

If it rains before seven
It will be fine before eleven.

A sunny shower
Won't last half an hour.

Evening red and morning grey promises a very fine day
Evening grey and morning red sends the shepherd wet to bed.

More rain, more rest
Fair weather not always best.

Gutch and Peacock add a few other random weather superstitions.[23] These include, 'If a cat washes over her ear, it is a sign of fine weather. When a dog or cat eats grass, it betokens approaching rain. When a swallow flies low, rain is at hand. Shooting stars are a sign of wind. When it rains with the wind in the east, it will rain for twenty-four hours at least.'

Some folk used a certain phrase to describe the lingering patches of snow under hedgerows. They called them 'dead men's bones' and the belief was that as long as they remained, more snow could be expected. The *Lincolnshire Poacher* magazine quotes a lovely snippet of what they call 'yellow-belly humour', concerning two Lincolnshire gentlemen discussing the weather: 'One said, "It's an owery owd mornin', 'Arry." "Aye, it is" replied the other. "My wireless sez rain. What's yars say?"'[24]

As well as the weather, the moon and the sun encouraged many superstitions as they had great influence upon the weather but also over crops, women and animals. For instance it was said that one should not kill a pig at the wane of the moon as it was bad luck, and meant the bacon would not swell in the pot. To see the moon reflected in a mirror was a sign that something would happen during the day to make you angry. At the new moon, girls would bind their eyes with a silken scarf and look up and count how many moons they could see. Whatever the number they counted represented the number of years they would have to wait until they married.

An old saying tells that mill stones should be set to 'turn with the sun, since the miller will never thrive while their course is against it.'[25] It was said also that if the sun shines on the apple trees on Christmas Day then there will be a heavy crop of fruit next season. However, when planting, 'Seed sown during a moon that came in on a Sunday and went out on a Sunday, will never come to much.'

Roy Fisk catalogues some old Lincolnshire remedies, but neither he nor I recommend the use of them if you find yourself troubled with any of the following![26] If you are afflicted with ague (a form of Malaria) then the old belief was to line your shoes with the leaves of a tansy plant and if this did not do the trick, pills of compressed spider's webs were suggested, to be taken before breakfast. If these are hard to come by, live spiders between two slices of bread and butter should do the trick. Think how jealous your work colleagues would be of your packed lunch! Another cure was to gather seven worms from the wet earth of a new grave, at midnight, and mix them into a paste, then apply. Take your pick!

To help stop the shakes of the ague one could tie a piece of hair to an aspen tree.

If bitten by a mad dog, you should apparently place in the bitten hand the key from the church door. Fits can allegedly be charmed away by touching or wearing a rope which has been used for hanging, or wearing a silver ring which has been made from money and consecrated at an altar. Those suffering from rheumatism should carry a potato in their pocket. Alternatively they can be cured by being confirmed a second time.

Cramp can be avoided by carrying a lucky bone in one's shoe, whose bone is not quite clear, or leaving a bowl of water under the bed, or even placing a piece of cork between the mattress and the bed. Also, if shoes are placed in the shape of a 'T' at the bottom of your bed when going to sleep at night, this will help with cramp. For scalds, a special chant is repeated whilst dressing the wound with bramble leaves dipped in spring water: 'There came three ladies out of the East. One with fire and two with frost. Out with the fire, in with the frost.'

When you are bothered by warts, place in a bag as many pebbles as you have warts and leave the bag at some crossroads. You will lose your warts but they will be transferred to the unfortunate person who picks up the bag. Or if you can sell them to a friend, wrap the money up and bury it and your warts should disappear. If this does not work, try to rub some dandelion juice into them, or the soft white insides of a broad bean pod. The remedy for boils is a salve of soft soap and sugar, fig poultices or buttermilk swallowed three times a day, whilst fasting. Jaundice is relieved by drinking a tea made from the twigs or bark of the barberry bush, or a mixture of sheep dung in boiled milk. Similarly, a concoction of sheep's dung and cream can be a cure for small pox.

A toothache can be cured by 'fill[ing] the mouth with cold water and sit[ting] on the fire until it boils, when the pain will be gone'. Either that or the pain of your burning behind will have distracted you from your tooth! If you carry the tip of a cow's boiled tongue in your pocket, you will be protected from the toothache coming on. If you have a headache, a recommended cure was to wrap the skin of a snake around your hat. It should relieve the pain. For sore eyes, wash them out with a concoction of eight garden snails shaken in a bottle with spring water.

For whooping cough you should wear shredded garlic inside your socks when you are in bed. This will keep those pesky vampires at bay as well! Alternatively, for children you could feed them fried mice, or let a horse breathe down their throat. If the child is having none of this, try hanging a bag of insects around the child's neck. Belief has it that the cough will disappear as the insects decay. A less gruesome answer would be to take three hairs from the cross on a donkey's back for your cure, or to ride a quarter of a mile upon a donkey.

If you have a cut from a knife or another piece of metal, to make the skin heal faster, clean and tend to the offending metal first, ridding it of any dirt or rust. Bleeding can be stopped by applying a thick cobweb. I have heard this to be true and believe it was a method used during battles centuries ago, however I would recommend using a bandage, if you have the choice!

The *Lincolnshire Poacher* magazine quotes from the *News Chronicle* of 1892,[27] which states that many a farm in Kesteven used to hang a mouldy Good Friday bun from the beams of the kitchen ceiling. The idea was that if someone in the family or even any of the cattle were suffering from certain ailments that a mouldy portion of the bun would be cut down and mashed into some water to create a remedy for the complaint. There are other incidents related of people using mouldy fruit or scraping the mould off hanging meat and wrapping the wound with the mouldy fat, and the idea that this cleaned out the wound and helped the healing process was prolific; a possible forerunner of penicillin perhaps.

Along with numerous superstitions and beliefs, Lincolnshire was full of its own sayings about every day things. For example someone away from home feeling homesick may say 'I wish I had hold of our cat's tail.' When changing underwear before leaving the house, people would say 'I must make a decent accident.' Something which was scarcely worth mentioning would be 'neither nowt n' summat'.

A charming saying from Alkborough was repeated to children who were being too nosy:

Clean and paid for
Washed and cared for
If you don't like it
What do you stare for?

These adages and practices, along with the wonderful Lincolnshire dialect, would fill many books, but for the study of folklore we have other matters to attend to.

# 8

# A LINCOLNSHIRE YEAR

For this chapter I have Maureen Sutton[1] to thank for much of the detailed and thorough information about the different festivals and rites of Lincolnshire throughout the year.

January brings the snow, makes the feet and fingers glow.

## 1 January

As in many other parts of the country, this day, First Footing, represented the belief that the very first person over the threshold of a house on New Year's Day brought with them either the good or bad luck for the rest of the year. Naturally, if the person brought bad news, then ill-luck would befall the house. The tradition dictated that a man with dark hair carrying a piece of wood, some coal and some silver would be the bearer of good luck. Fair or ginger hair was seen as bad luck, but a woman was worse still! Gutch and Peacock, however, tell of a tradition in Lincolnshire Marsh where a light-haired man with a fair complexion was preferred.[2]

Sutton offers a few possible explanations for this tradition. One theory is that when the Vikings invaded the county they raped many of the indigenous women and so it was seen as very bad luck to open the door to a fair-haired man. Silver could be viewed as a good charm for the year's fortunes and coal brought with it a warm house. Wood could have signified averting death, as bringing in wood ensured a coffin was not carried out that year.

Ethel Rudkin relates the ritual a lady of Caistor performed every New Year's Day.[3] She would arrange for a man to enter her house first thing in the morning, carrying something yellow, such as jasmine. He was instructed to go to the fire and stir it up with the poker whilst wishing her a happy New Year. She said that the stirring of the ashes was a sign of stirring a good friendship and making it glow again.

The first day in January was also viewed as a 'no washing day', as it signalled a death within the family before spring and thus was avoided:

> If you wash on New Year's Day, you'll wash one of the family away.

There used to be a tradition in Lincoln, early in January, of hosting a feast for all the poor children of the city, named the Robin Dinner. Hundreds of poor children would be gathered for a hearty meal at the Drill Hall, where festivities and entertainment followed. Unfortunately this is said to have died out by the late 1930s.

Rudkin mentions a tradition of the 'Plough Jags' doing the rounds on the first Monday in January.[4] She states that this was the only night of the year where there was no law and so they could not be 'had up'. The tradition was that gangs of ploughboys visited each house in their area asking for money. If anyone refused they would have a furrow ploughed on the path before their door. They are also referred to as 'Plough Jacks' or 'Plough Bullocks' and are said to have dressed as morris dancers and performed little plays.

## 5 January

Lincolnshire, having a very large farming community, had a great many superstitions concerning crops, as they represented the livelihood of so many. The 'Shooting of Trees' was one such rite performed to ensure a good crop for the year. This involved visiting the orchards and shooting at the trees in order to get their sap flowing – then a good harvest would be guaranteed. This is a similar rite to the Wassailing in which the southern folk of the country participated to ensure a good crop of cider apples for next year's harvest.

## 6 January

This date marks the occasion of the famous Haxey Hood game. This is a tradition which has stood the test of time and even though it is a very old ritual, having being practised since the thirteenth century, it is still as popular as ever today. The precise origin of the game is somewhat unclear but one story tells of an elderly lady, possibly Lady Mowbray, Lady of the Manor, who was travelling one windy twelfth night when her red hood was blown off over the fields by a strong gust. A handful of villagers who were working nearby chased it, and after much fun and excitement returned the hood to its owner. The story tells that the actual man who caught the hood was too shy to give it back and so another handed it over to Lady Mowbray. She was so grateful and amused, she gave thirteen half acres of land, Haxey Fields, to twelve men, for an annual celebration of the fun, and she apparently called the shy man 'fool', hence this character in the games. The whereabouts of twelve of the half acres' is now unknown, but the last half is used in the Haxey Hood today.

The game today requires a 'hood', twelve 'boggons' and a 'fool'. The boggons, or 'plough-boggons' as they are sometimes referred to, are dressed in red jackets and represent the original twelve who first caught the stray hood. In the week leading up to the game, the twelve boggons journey around the village and visit all the inhabitants, inviting them to attend the game, as players or observers, and to gather funds for beer and entertainment.

On the day itself, at around one in the afternoon, the players gather by the churchyard and the fool gives a speech about the game's rules and announces which pub is offering the most beer for the final catcher of the hood. The fool is also entitled to kiss any one he pleases, even 'be she the highest i' the land'.[5]

Elaine Kazimierczuk inquired what qualifications were needed for the job of the fool and was given the answer; 'You just need tolerance, fortitude and a capacity to drink beer'.[6]

The stone depicted here, outside St Nicholas' Church, Haxey, is known as the Mowbray Stone, on which the fool stands when delivering the introduction to the game.

A LINCOLNSHIRE YEAR 155

Photograph of the fool at the Haxey Hood celebration. (Kindly donated by Arthur Franks.)

The vast numbers attracted to the Haxey Hood annual event. (Kindly donated by Arthur Franks.)

Then to the Haxey Field, where the eldest boggon throws the hood high into the air. The idea is that the players must try and capture the hood and carry it out of the field, whilst the boggons fight to keep it within the bounds. If the boggons succeed until evening, they can retire and the players play on down the streets, fighting for which pub the hood will be taken to. Once there, it is kept by the landlord until next year and everyone has a good old knees-up. The merriment lasts a few more days and originally there was the tradition of 'Smoking the Fool', whereby a fire was made beneath the fool, who sat in a large tree and then was suspended from a branch and dipped into the thick smoke emanating from the crackling damp straw.

Many believe the game is linked to the ancient festival of John Barleycorn – or the Green King, as the song 'John Barleycorn' is ritually sung. These are ancient traditions of fertility and the cycle of the year, certainly apt for a farming community. Jeremy Hobson has another similar theory: 'In Viking culture a bull was often sacrificed at this time of year and its head (hood?) was used as a sort of football in the hope that its blood would ensure a good growing season.'[7]

## 6 January

There is an annual banquet on this date, named the Lincoln Cake Ball. It has been held every year since 1795, apart from during the two world wars. Held in the County Assembly Rooms in Bailgate, it is a dinner to which one has to have an invitation from the mayor.

Plough Sunday and Monday were the first Sunday and Monday after twelfth night and were a farming tradition to bless the plough. It was decorated and paraded around the village.

## 20 January

The eve of the feast of St Agnes, the patron saint of girls, falls on this day. There used to be an important tradition for young women to use this night to perform certain rituals in order to catch sight of their future husbands. For example, girls would sow barley seeds under trees and chant:

> Barley, barley, I sow thee
> That my true-love I may see;
> Take thy rake and follow me.

If performed correctly, the girls should then dream of their betrothed that night.

## 26 January

This date signifies a more modern Lincolnshire festival, the Lincoln Australian Breakfast. This tradition began due to a visit the mayor took to Australia in 1991. On this day there is a huge breakfast situated on the beach with people dressed up and some in costume. The mayor was so taken with the idea that he brought it home to Lincoln. On the Sunday nearest to the 26th, the Lawn Centre now holds a breakfast celebration for up to 1,600 people, with Australian music, dress and custom being the order of the day.

## 2 February

> 'A February spring is worth nothing.'

February is the month for the farmers to clean out ditches and get ready for the year ahead but there was always a fear that if it was a warm February that things would come into flower early and then be killed off by a later cold snap, hence the saying above. Along with this was the idea that if it was warm enough for 'the gnats [to] fly in February the farmer will beg at Harvest'.

Candlemas, the midpoint of winter, is a traditional Christian festival, to celebrate the purification of Mary, forty days after the birth of Jesus. It was a time to bless the candles in a commemoration of the return of the light. As with other counties, Lincolnshire celebrated this day with candle processions, feasting and horse trading. One of the old beliefs was that the candles blessed at Candlemas held such special properties that they could help cure illnesses. For example, if someone had a sore throat they should lay the blessed candles in a cross shape across the afflicted throat and they should be cured.

## 14 February

Again as in all counties, this day is celebrated by lovers, and in Lincolnshire in particular people used Valentine's Day to perform a number of rituals to determine their future partners. For instance, one could tie a strand of hair through a ring and sleep with it under the pillow in order to dream of a future spouse. In Gainsborough there was a custom of pinning five bay leaves to your pillow, one at each corner and then one in the middle, in the belief you would then dream of your husband to be. In Coningsby, bachelors would wear a small yellow flower upon their lapels to let the ladies know they were available. Wearing one would signify the prediction that you would soon be married. Tradition also spoke of the idea that the first unmarried man a girl saw that morning would be the one they would marry – and too bad if it was someone they disliked!

The sending of a valentine was popular too, as Gutch and Peacock show us with an example of a ditty:

If you love me, love me true;
Send me a ribbon, and let it be blue.
If you hate me let it be seen;
Send me a ribbon, and let it be green.[8]

## 29 February

The country over this was the day when it was seen as acceptable for the lady to ask the man to marry her. In Boston it was a known tradition that if a girl leapt onto a man's back it was her way of proposing and no words were needed. To agree, the man would then leap on her back. This could be due to the term 'Leap Year'. If a man refused the proposal, some traditions said he must buy the lady a silk dress in recompense. As Sutton points out, although an expense, this was a much cheaper option.

## 21 March

March comes in like a lion, goes out like a lamb.

It was often believed that if there was bad weather at the beginning of this month then it would improve, bringing milder conditions by late March and into April.

This day marks the celebration of the first day of spring. The Lincolnshire tradition was to throw clods of earth across the fields to awaken the sleeping spirits in the earth. The four corners represented the four compass points and sowing and planting for the year began. The River Trent, which flows into the Humber twenty miles away, feels the equinox effects of the tidal bore, also known as the 'Aegir', after the Norse God of the sea. Felt also at Gainsborough, there was once a custom of throwing a piece of silver into the water at high spring tide as a toll, to prevent ever drowning there and also to soothe the fury of the flow.

The 'Lincolnshire Handicap' horserace, starting in 1849 in Lincoln, was a very popular event, lasting until the 1960s. It was then moved to the Doncaster course and is still the first major race of the flat racing season today.

## 29 March

This is Thomas Kendall Day, named after the vicar of Louth in 1534, who opposed the Dissolution of the Monasteries. He was part of the Pilgrimage of Grace rebellion, which unfortunately failed, and he was hanged in 1537. Lincoln Cathedral commemorates his death every year with a service on his anniversary.

## Spring Cleaning

This was once a mammoth event, taking place sometime between February and Easter, whereby the whole contents of the house were cleaned and every household took part in this annual ritual. Every curtain was taken down and washed; carpets were taken outside and beaten; rooms whitewashed, painted and redecorated. It was such an important tradition that people would not enter one another's houses until it had been done. Since the modern inventions of vacuum cleaners and washing machines, cleaning is much easier and done much more regularly, thus the need for this huge upheaval is lessened, yet still we use the phrase 'spring cleaning' whenever we do a good clear out.

## Brusting Saturday

As a movable event, this took place on the Saturday before Shrove Tuesday. A special cake was made, rather like a pancake but thicker and more crumbly, made with oat flour. The cakes were called 'brustins' and were often served with honey poured across although some people ate them with fish. Eggs were once forbidden during Lent so these cakes and pancakes were a good way of eating them up. The money saved on buying eggs for the next six weeks was given to the poor. Many towns in the country had a pancake bell and in Lincolnshire this was apparently rung as a signal for housewives to begin to prepare their pancake batter.

An indication of how cold this time of year was then (and can still be today); one popular batter recipe included two tablespoons of freshly fallen snow. When added right at the end, this was thought to make the batter light. The first pancake tossed would traditionally be fed to the cock as a reminder that Peter denied Jesus three times before the cock crowed. The daughter of the house watched this custom closely, as the number of hens that arrived to help the cock eat it signified the number of years she would remain unwed.

At one time it was also the tradition to give school children an orange on Shrove Tuesday, hence the use of the name Orange Day. Certain places used to have a game, the Lug and Bite game, on this day, whereby children would crowd around the schoolmaster whilst he threw an orange up into the air. The child who caught it took a bite and then had to throw it back up. If he kept hold, taking more than one bite, the other children were allowed to lug (pull) his hair and ears until he threw it up again.

## Mothering Sunday

Once also known as 'Refreshment Sunday' as it was used as a break from the abstinence of Lent. Another name was Simnel Sunday, after a traditional, rich almond cake. Thick almond paste was spread in the middle and on the top, along with eleven small balls, to represent the apostles (barring Judas) and also the number of months the girls were away from home in the days when the roads were bad and transport was poor. They often had to work in another town but came home on Mothering Sunday, which was like a family reunion day.

## Mid-Lent Fair

Apparently originating over a thousand years ago, this fair, often held during the week after Mothering Sunday, appears in Stamford. Now more of a funfair than the market it used to be, it moves on to Grantham the week after and then heads north for the summer. Some say it is now the largest street fair in Lincolnshire. The town mayor opens the festivities and rings the Mid-Lent Fair bell to announce the start of the six-day event.

## Caistor Gad-Whip on Palm Sunday

This is now a lost custom but was very popular through the 1800s. A gad-whip is a long whip used by ploughmen to drive their oxen faster. Every Palm Sunday the 10-foot gad-whip was cracked three times in the church porch by the Lord of the Manor of Hundon. Apparently, the first time was for the first lesson of Easter, then the second after the second lesson, involving a purse with thirty pieces of silver. The custom ceased in 1846 but one possible explanation for the tradition was that it was penance for the accidental death of a boy by the Lord of the Manor and this personal act became bound up with the tenure of the land. There was controversy at the time, some people saying it was an indecent act to perform in the church, whilst others argued it was in keeping with the Easter theme. The thirty coins were symbolic of Judas' betrayal and the cracking of the whip three times was a reminder of the cock crowing and Peter's denial. The controversy seemed to fuel interest and at the 1843 service over a hundred people turned up to see the curious custom.

If you ever hear any of the older generation in Lincolnshire call a child with a dirty face a 'Molly Grime' it is a reference to a very old tradition linked to Good Friday. The washing of an effigy of the dead Christ was a tradition every Good Friday, along with littering his bier with flowers. 'Malgraen' meant 'holy image washing', but became corrupted to Molly Grime.

Good Friday was also the day for baking hot cross buns and as it is a 'holy' day, the buns are said to contain magical properties. The *Lincolnshire Life* magazine tells

The gad-whip, preserved in a glass case on the wall of the church of St Peter and St Paul, Caister.

An effigy of Mary supporting the dead Jesus, over the porch entrance of St Peter's Church, Glentham. The tradition of washing the image of Christ was once held here. This is thought to be the only remaining effigy of Mary holding Jesus' body left in Lincolnshire and one of very few left in the country after the Reformation.

of a woman from Lincoln who held that one should always bake thirteen buns, keeping one back in case anyone in the family should become ill during the year.[9] If they do, the idea was to scrape some of the top off the bun, add it to a glass of warm milk and drink it before bed. By the morning the illness should have disappeared.

Even though it was taboo for women to do any washing or housework on Good Friday, it was apparently seen as a lucky day for farmers to plant their potatoes. Another Lincolnshire belief was that any person born on a Good Friday could not be frightened.

In the 1920s and '30s, people believed that the sun danced on Easter morning and could forecast the weather for the rest of the year. A bucket of water was placed outside and as the sun rose it reflected upon the surface of it. It would 'wap and wade' which, when translated, meant that if it rippled it was meant to be a sign that there would be enough water all summer but if the sun moved slowly across the water it was expected to be a very dry summer.

Tansy pudding was a traditional dish for Easter Day, eaten with orange marmalade, supposed to represent the bitter herbs eaten with the paschal lamb.

Children were involved in egg-rolling competitions on Easter Monday, rolling hard-boiled eggs down hills to see which survived the longest. This was a symbol of the rolling away of the stone across Jesus' tomb.

Hare Pie was a traditional dish for Easter Monday, constituting hare, hard-boiled eggs and a pastry case. There was a well-known practice at Hare Hill, near Louth, where such a pie made by the wife of the vicar was cut up and distributed to the gathered crowd.

Rudkin mentions a custom that was practiced every Easter in Bourne since 1770, the Meadow Letting custom.[10] A Mr Clay apparently gave a piece of land, White Bread Meadow, to the inhabitants on the condition that the rent was used for charitable purposes. Further conditions stipulated that two good loads of manure should be put on the land and that the bush in the middle of the field should not be cut or damaged, by man nor beast. Apparently, although the original is now gone, replacement bushes have always been planted. To decide who rented the land from year to year, a race was run by a number of boys. Once they were off the bidding began in the auction and as the race finished, the last person to bid had the lease for that year. After the bidding there was a feast of bread, cheese and spring onions. The race held today is more of a token of what was intended but the results of the auction are still legally binding.

Gutch and Peacock mention a game celebrated on the Tuesday a fortnight after Easter Sunday, called Holk.[11] Girls and boys would catch each other as they passed on the streets and refuse to let them go unless they paid a small fee. This money was then spent on a feast in the evening and great fun was said to be had by both parties, both day and evening.

Another moveable custom was to welcome the cuckoo, when it was first heard in the year, with a special cuckoo ale. It was also customary for girls to count the number of times it cuckooed, which signalled the number of years they would have to wait to be wed.

## 1 April

When April blows his horn 'tis good for hay and corn.

April Fool's Day was celebrated only half the day. People, children especially, would play tricks on each other all morning but if someone played a trick in the afternoon the common retort would be, 'April Fool's Day passed and gone and you're the fool for making me one'. Widdowson[12] relates one particular trick a lady from Louth remembers from her childhood: 'We always got a small piece of coal wrapped in a toffee paper in our lunch. Believe me, we should have been very disappointed if it had not been there!'

## 6 April

Known as Flitting Day, whereby all the farm workers and their families moved from their tied cottages to a new place of work. It was also the day they paid up the year's rent. One theory for it occurring at this time of year is that it was near the equinox, the time many ancient cultures viewed as the start of the New Year. Flitting Day was an immense day for mothers, whose responsibility it was to get everything spick and span in the house for the newcomers. It was, however, seen as unlucky to move house on a Friday, so if the 6th fell on a Friday, people would wait another day to move.

## April Pleasure Fair

An annual event held in Lincoln, this fair takes place on the South Common. It has been running for years and Sutton includes some memories from people who attended the fair in the early 1900s. There was dancing and stages with music, a variety of food on sale, coconut shies, shooting galleries, side shows such as a snake woman or the world's fattest man, performing fleas, boxing matches, up and down horses, waltzers, swing yachts, cake walks, strong man acts, and more. The fair today is very similar apart from having a more modern, updated feel and faster rides!

## Lincoln Horse Fair

Another event that was held for centuries, this was a huge affair, spreading out over all the streets, with hundreds of different horses stationed all across the town. It lasted a full week, at the end of April, and was massively popular but died out in the 1950s due to the increase in motorised vehicles and farming machinery. Enormous crowds would gather, with people travelling from all over the country and so the inns and pubs all did a good trade that week as well as the ice-cream sellers and hot pea stalls. Even those not interested in buying a horse were attracted, and one girl Sutton mentions remembers her mother taking her along for the chance they might be given some free cabbages at the end of the day. Farmer's apparently used to give away cabbages and other vegetables that the horses had not eaten, as it was easier than carting them all back home again.

## 24 April

St Mark's Eve involved many different rituals connected with divining a future spouse. One such custom was for three girls to gather together and bake a dumb cake, in complete silence. The cake had to be prepared by midnight, for as the clock struck twelve each of the girls would tear themselves off a piece and eat it. Still silent, they would then walk backwards up the stairs to bed and if all was done correctly they were to see a shadow of their future husband following them up the stairs. One condition stated that they must get into bed before the shadow reached them.

For those who saw no shadow, a knocking sound may be heard on the door or a rustling in the house and this would reassure them they were still to find husbands – but the poor girl who was destined never to marry would neither see nor hear anything and may even have terrible dreams of death. As can be imagined, this practice lost popularity during the war years as so many young men were killed and thus the girls viewed it as a futile event.

## May Day

> Wash your face in the May morning dew, and you will have a fair face.

May Day is now the nearest Monday to the first of the month; it used to be the nearest Sunday. There are a host of traditional celebrations, including dancing around the maypole, processions, the crowning of the May Queen and prank playing.

'Maying' was a custom whereby the children of the village would visit all the houses with seasonal flowers and extract money and gifts from the residents. It was performed as a ritual to welcome in the May and the spring, and the garlands were made in a traditional oval shape, with dolls placed in the middle. The children were often given a few coppers, or if they were in short supply a pin to give their mothers. It was viewed as bad luck, however, to take the May blossom inside the house, which Sutton suggests could have been linked to the Catholic tradition of placing garlands in front of the statue of Mary. During the Reformation this was forbidden and could even result in death, and so people avoided the act.

Maypole dancing was also a popular tradition during May and this is a fine example of a village maypole, seen in Hemswell, along Maypole Street.

May dancing was also a tradition. Morris men would welcome in the new month by dancing in the four corners of Lincoln; west, north, east and south. They had a 5 a.m. start on the 1 May and the bells they wore and sticks they knocked together were all tools with which to drive away the evil spirits from the city.

Morris dancers also participate at the May Day Lincoln Folk Festival, which is a three-day event, first beginning in 1983. This event was linked to the Lincoln Arts Festival but soon became an occasion in its own right, involving many local and national folk musicians.

May is a month of flowers and there are many festivals celebrating the different flowers of the county, such as cowslips, lilies, tulips and blossom – all linked to this particular season and to the symbol of new life.

## 11 – 5 May

It was once custom to eat rook pie during this month on Rook Sunday, as the baby rooks venturing from their nests for the first time were easy pickings to catch. The pastry around the edge of the pie was marked using the feet of the rooks and some people would even serve their pie with the legs of the rook sticking up out of the middle.

## 14 May

Known as Pag Rag Day, this was the day that all the servants used to return home with all their dirty washing packed into white linen bags, known as pag bags.

This date was also known as Hiring Fair, as traditionally it was the day when farm workers were hired. The employers would know what jobs the men were looking for and which skills they possessed just by looking at what clothes they wore on this day and the tools they carried with them. When a deal was struck, the farmer would give the worker a shilling, known as a 'fastening penny', as a term of employment and then they would be paid a penny per month thereafter. Rudkin says that Brigg had the wonderful incentive of offering the first man to arrive in town, who was looking for work, a free pint.[13] As one can imagine, this became very competitive and men would be rolling up at five in the morning.

## 24 May

Lincolnshire is well known for the Wesley family, who resided at Epworth Rectory, the sons, John and Charles, well-known preachers in the 1730s. This date is known as Wesley Day, and they are remembered annually during the communion service in Lincoln Cathedral.

'Beating the Bounds' was an old tradition used in many counties, Lincolnshire included, before accurate maps were produced. Where there might be disputes

Remembrance stone for John Wesley, founder of Methodism, situated in Wroot, where he served as curate for two years.

over the boundaries people would go out and beat down growth and mark the soil to show the younger generations where the boundaries were. Bourne Abbey Church is one of the few places left that still marks the tradition by taking people from the parish out, in May, and walking the boundary paths.

Boston May Fair was a large horse, cattle and sheep market but was also known as something of a pleasure fair, where even quack doctors would attend, selling their herbal medicines and remedies. It is still a popular event today, though more of a pleasure fair than anything.

## 12 June

A dripping June brings all things into tune.

This day in June is known as John Dalderby Day. He was a Lincolnshire man, born in Horncastle; he went on to become the Bishop of Lincoln in 1300. He died in 1320 but a number of miracles were accredited to him, such as curing the people of Rutland who had become unable to speak and were only able to bark. He is remembered in a service every 12 June in Lincoln Cathedral.

## 17 June

The Feast of St Botolph was held on this day. The people of Boston claimed him as their founder and the Boston Stump is dedicated to him. He died in 608 and at one time there used to be a twenty-five day fair held in his memory. He is also now remembered annually in a service in Lincoln Cathedral.

The 'Lincoln Show', which began in 1819, is still going strong today and attracts thousands of people from all around the country. It is primarily an agricultural show, usually held towards the end of the third week in June.

## 23 – 25 June

The Stow Green Fair was another huge event attended by thousands. It was a horse and wool fair which started in the 1200s and retained its popularity until the 1950s. It is thought that fairs were held here even before that date, as it is also the feast day of Etheldreda, to whom the Stow minster is dedicated, who died 23 June 679.

Late in June the Horncastle to Skegness Walk used to take place, which was a twenty-four-mile fun walk, started in 1903. A band was present and competitions and prizes were on offer, one of which was auctioned off in 2010; a bronze medallion, won by W.S. Williams, who completed the walk in three hours and thirty-four minutes in 1903.

An information board now stands at the site of the Stow Green Fair, showing photographs of the horse fair from 1908. A little tricky to find, it is north of the village of Stow, just off the A52 towards Threekingham. The board is beside the road at the T-junction between Mareham Lane and Stow Lane.

## Crop Gathering in July

When bracken is down in July it means that there will be a hard winter.

July was very busy for the people of the land, whose time was taken up with crop gathering and hay making and so there was not much time for celebration during this month. But in the 1940s, it became the tradition that during the last week of July and the first week of August, the workers could have an annual holiday, named Trip Weeks. Many of the factories closed altogether during these weeks and even organised bus trips so the people could get away. The seaside, of course, was the most popular destination, Skegness and Mablethorpe being favourites.

In the 1920s and '30s there was a tradition named the Monkey Walk Parade held on Sunday afternoons in July, involving the youth of Lincoln who would dress in their Sunday best and parade up and down the high street. Men would take one side of the street and ladies the other and they would watch each other as they walked past. It was a gentle form of courtship and many couples would become paired up as a result. The tradition is still remembered now, when people don their best clothes and refer to them as their monkey suit.

## Gainsborough Co-op Gala Day

This started in 1905 and was held on the first Saturday in July. This day was organised for the children of members of the Gainsborough Co-op and a variety of games were organised for them to enjoy. Rather like children's sports days today, they were encouraged to join in relay races, sack races, sprint races and egg and spoon. There was dancing, a Punch and Judy show, a beauty queen contest and many other activities for children to enjoy.

## 6 July

Barton Bike Night is a relatively new event, having run for the last fifteen years. The village becomes packed full of stalls, food and drink, as well as hosting a variety of bike-related events. All kinds of motorbikes turn up and there is so much to watch, with all the trailing and ride-outs – certainly not one to miss!

In mid-July there was a nine-day long festival at Stamford, boasting crafts, music, floats, sporting activities, children's games and a flea market. Today the festival takes the form of a parade, with floats and a procession to join in with.

## 22 – 24 July

The So Festival takes place on these days. Started in 2009, this is a relatively new festival but proves to be very popular. There is street theatre, music, comedy, carnivals, dancing and much more.

## 24 July

In 1971, Bardney saw its very own folk festival. The locals were all rather worried about it before the event, thinking it would be a noisy, messy, bad idea with lots of people causing trouble, but the whole thing went off without a hitch. Approximately 60,000 people turned up, some travelling from Australia and it was a peaceful, successful event, but only ever repeated once, in 1999.

## Samphire Day

> In April he [the cuckoo] opens his bill, in May he sings all day, in June he changes his tune, in July away he does fly, in August go he must.

The first Monday in August is known in the south of Lincolnshire, Holbeach and the Wash area as Samphire Day. Samphire is a plant which grows well in marshland areas and is also known as the poor man's asparagus. This day was a day's holiday for the locals, who would use it to go and pick the plants and pickle them. They made a real occasion out of the day, taking a picnic along, and some people took an oil stove to brew up tea. It is said that it is a favourite taste of Prince Charles and it is still picked and pickled today, then apparently sold to Harrods in London.

Sheep shearing was a very important event in late July/early August, where all the men would work in teams and visit each other's farms to help one another get all the sheep done. A supper of frumenty, a meal using eggs and wheat and sometimes dried fruit, was enjoyed at the end of the day; a wholesome meal meant to give them energy for the task in hand. The Lincolnshire men had a special way to count sheep:

1: yan
2: tan
3: tethera
4: pethera
5: pimp
6: sethera
7: lethera
8: overa
9: covera
10: dic

Thought to be a link to their Celtic origins, a similar system was used by the Welsh and Cornish shepherds.

## 6 August

The annual Brigg Fair was a popular horse fair in its time but like many others began to lose popularity with the increase of motorised vehicles. It is, however, still celebrated today, if not quite in the same way. Many markets take place including livestock, and some people do still bring their horse and carts to parade the grounds.

## Horncastle and the Great August Horse Fair

This was once a huge three-week long affair. Begun in 1229, it is thought to have been the largest of its kind at one time and people from all over the world would travel to it. Brass bands would march the streets and the town would be crammed with people of every class. This fair was last held in 1948.

August and September were the main months for gathering in the harvest and so there were numerous rituals surrounding these months as there were many farming communities in Lincolnshire. One widespread custom was, once the last load was ready the women and children would ride it home and if there were any early apples, the children were each given one as a treat.

Women and children used to go out 'gleaning', which was a tradition of collecting the leftover crops from farmers' fields after the harvest had been collected. The practice could be viewed as an early form of welfare but it was also a social occasion, with the youngsters competing to see who could get the fullest sack load. In many parishes there was a gleaning bell, which was rung to call the gleaners into the fields when the main harvest was completed and then to call them home again in the evening. There were known signs that a field was not ready to be gleaned as yet, such as a sheaf on the gate. The vicar of the villages would collect some corn and wheat from each farmer and these tithe profits were often used for welfare purposes.

Cock Stack was a well-known practice, whereby a large cock was created out of straw and wood when the harvest was finished, and was placed on top of the last stack as an advert to everyone for miles around that the farmer had wheat for sale.

There were many songs to keep people's spirits up while working and, of course, when the harvest was over there were songs of celebration:

> I rent my shirt and tore my skin
> To get my master's harvest in.
> Hip, hip, hurrah!
> Harvest in and harvest home,
> We'll have a good fat hen and bacon bone.[14]

## 24 August

St Bartholomew's Day Knives was a tradition whereby men would give each other knives on this date and even the headmaster of the school would give some to lads who had been good. St Bartholomew was apparently murdered with a knife and so the knife is his symbol. Sutton also links the St Bartholomew's Day massacre to the symbol of the knife. The knives given on this day were called lamb's foot knives as they were often small enough to remove small stones or cut rough edges from a lamb's foot.

## 3 September

The Lincoln Long-Wool Ram Sale was a sheep farmers' fair for the buying and selling of all things to do with sheep. Folk in Lincolnshire are still very proud of their sheep and they can often be seen displayed at agricultural shows and fairs around the country.

September was also the month for the gathering and drying of herbs and the last of the onions, ready for the winter months. Lavender was popular for use in pillows and for easing headaches; onions were used as a cure for chilblains and colds; thyme, sage, rosemary and many others were collected, each having their own uses.

As in all farming communities, most of the corn should have been harvested by September and so large harvest suppers and celebrations took place during this month. Lincolnshire, of course, excelled in this tradition, having so many families and communities linked to farming, and the feasting, dancing and singing involved everyone.

## 8 September

This date saw the ancient tradition of the Grimsby Boar Hunt, whereby the annual sport of boar hunting commenced and landowners presented a boar's head to the mayor, resulting in a huge final feast. The HMS *Grimsby* uses the emblem of a boar for the ship's crest, as a remembrance of this ancient right allowing the townsfolk to hunt boar in Bradley Woods, nearby. Whether the tradition will be reignited with the supposed increase of wild boar in Britain, only time will tell.

## 14 September

Once known as Fool's Fair, this was held in Broadgate, Lincoln. It was an annual fair held for the sale of cattle and apparently granted to the people by King William as he and his wife visited the town and gave the people an offer of a favour of their choosing. He apparently granted their request for a fair with a smile, as he viewed it as a humble request indeed.

## 29 September

This was Michaelmas Day, customarily the date when farm and agricultural workers moved to new employment.

## 1 October

Each leaf caught as it falls in October means a happy month in the coming year.

Lincolnshire Day: although only first held officially in 2006, the date marks the anniversary of the Lincolnshire Rising in 1536, when the Catholics revolted against the establishment of Henry VIII's Church of England. It is the day when all things Lincolnshire are celebrated; from historical events, traditions, culture, present-day practices and, of course, food. Well known for its sausages, cheese, beer and other delights, this is the perfect day to celebrate them.

The Harvest Festival also took place on this day, where fruit and vegetables were displayed in the churches, people donating what they could, and then the goods were distributed to hospitals, the poor and the needy.

October was the month in which many village fairs, feasts and fêtes were once held, as all the harvest work was finished and people had some money to spend. It was a time for relaxation and fun and also the time when those who had left home for work elsewhere were allowed back for the weekend, for their own village feast. Much traditional fare was on offer along with fairground attractions which included rides, stalls and fortune tellers. Some villages also incorporated ploughing matches into their festivities.

Potato picking was of great importance and up until the 1950s, children were given an annual holiday during the potato harvest. In the 1920s and '30s many French and Irish labourers came to Lincolnshire looking for work. It was hard, back-breaking work in cold and wet conditions, with poor pay, but even so, women and children would help out for a bit of pocket money, in order to buy clothes for the winter.

The October Lincolnshire Stuff Ball, originating in 1785, was once an annual event, involving any locally produced materials, or 'stuff'. A feast with local food was on offer and those women who attended dressed in locally-made clothes would gain entrance for free. Every year there was a different colour code for the ball and thus the event was sometimes referred to as the Colour Fancy Dress Ball. It is said that upwards of 300 people attended, attired in garments manufactured from wool of the county.

## 31 October

Celebrated the country over, All Hallow's Eve is considered a very eerie night; the night when the lost souls returned to earth. This was the night people would gather round the fire and tell each other ghost stories, scare each other and share riddles. There were many rituals about how to catch sight of the Devil on this night, where to go and what one must do. Some villages had gatherings for the children to enjoy, with games such as bob the apple, hunt the thimble and blind man's buff. People would make lanterns from mangolds as we do nowadays with pumpkins. Hot baked potatoes, sausages and peas were the order of the day. Snap dragon was a local dish some people liked to include, containing lots of meat and brandy-soaked raisins, which were set alight for extra fun.

The *Lincolnshire Life* magazine shares an old superstition from Horsington, where at midnight on Halloween twelve lights were said to have been seen to rise from the mound in the churchyard where the ancient church of Horsington once stood.[15]

All that remains of the ancient church of Horsington, where strange lights were said to emerge. It is hidden amongst a thick clump of trees across a farmer's field next to Grange Farm, just outside Horsington, along Hale Road, from Stixwould.

They were apparently blue lights, split into groups of three which then travelled to the nearby villages of Horsington, Stixwould, Bucknall and Wadingworth. What these strange lights represented and when they were last observed is unknown, but if you are brave enough to search them out, this is the night to see them.

## 1 November

The religious observance of All Saints' Day. The following day is All Souls' Day, when Christians remembered their dead. On this day there was once a tradition, in Lincolnshire, of 'souling', whereby the children would go from house to house in the village, singing a ditty in order to receive a 'soul cake', which was a sort of bun.

## 3 November

Stickney Feast used to have a game called 'pelting the pig', whereby you could win a pig, which was a great prize one could put away ready for Christmas. Other prizes included a sack of potatoes or a joint of beef. There were a variety of different games played on this feast day.

## 4 November

'Guying' was a tradition where children would dress up in old clothes and masks and make an effigy of a guy, from straw and scraps of clothes, to take round with them. They would then visit houses in the village and were rewarded with coppers for reciting ditties such as:

Please to remember
The fifth of November
The poor old guy.
A hole in his stocking
A hole in his shoe,
Please can you spare him
A copper or two?
If you haven't got a penny
A half-penny will do
If you haven't got an half-penny
Well, God bless you.

## 5 November

Remember, remember the fifth of November! Guy and his companion's plot: We're going to blow the Parliament up! By God's mercy we wase catcht, with a dark lantern an' lighted matcht!

Bonfire Night. As in most places around the country, the custom was to collect together things to burn, from branches to old chairs – with a straw and paper guy effigy to burn on top, as a remembrance of Guy Fawkes who tried to blow up parliament during the Gun Powder Plot of 1605.

Lincolnshire, like all the counties, celebrated Bonfire Night and Mischief Night and Sutton gives a few examples of some of the mischievous acts in which the locals would take part. For example, one source told how they used to tie a button to a piece of cotton and attach it to someone's window, then jiggle the cotton so that it would continuously knock against the glass. Another trick was to tie two door handles together so people could not get out of their houses. Another popular one was to knock on a house door and then to run away before it was answered.

## 11 November

'Martinmas', rather like Flitting Day, was the date on which certain groups of farm labourers from areas of North Lincolnshire preferred to move, rather than the April date.

## 13 November

St Brice's Day, the Stamford Bull Running. St Brice's Day is the anniversary of the massacre of the Danes in 1002, and there is the possible connection here between blood spill and blood sport. The bull-running tradition involves the taunting and chasing of a bull through the streets of Stamford by a crowd of jeering men, women and children and packs of hunting dogs, until the bull eventually gives up, exhausted, and is then killed and roasted in a feast for the village. The whole process is rather savage and the tradition, fortunately now obsolete, met with much opposition through the years, especially from those who were members of the Society for the Prevention of Cruelty to Animals. The last time it took place was the late 1830s but the memory of the events still live on in the town even up to the present day.

One possible origin of the tradition stems from the tale of two fighting bulls being discovered in a field by some butchers. The men apparently tried to separate the bulls but their efforts accidentally resulted in both bulls running into the public highway. They then charged wildly into the town, spreading panic and alarm, until the Earl of Warren gave chase on his horse, joined by all the stray dogs in the area and brought the beasts to bay. The people apparently so enjoyed the 'sport' that the earl granted the town a meadow in which a bull fight could take place every year preceded by a bull chase through the town. November being such a cold month the idea of a race and then a huge feast was welcomed by the people and the locals thoroughly enjoyed the festivities, even until the last. Perhaps this is why the memory is still so strong.

## 17 November

This day is the Feast of St Hugh, who is the patron saint of Lincoln, the protector of sick children. He was the Bishop of Lincoln between 1186 and 1200 and his shrine in the cathedral became a very popular pilgrimage location. The feast used to be a thirty-day event, attracting many, and he is still remembered today within a service in Lincoln Cathedral on this date. This is a principle feast in the cathedral and is an occasion when the entire Foundation gathers to celebrate the Eucharist at midday.

## 30 November

This day or the nearest Sunday to it, usually the first Sunday in advent, was known in some areas as Stir Up Sunday, after the first words of the collect in the Book of Common Prayer, 'Stir up, we beseech Thee, O Lord, the wills of thy faithful people.'[16]

It was also the day many women in the county made their Christmas puddings, which should traditionally be stirred by all members of the household. One of the main ingredients was brandy, and as well as stopping any mould growing this helped to mature the pudding until Christmas.

## 10 December

In 1573 the borough of Boston was granted the right to hold an annual eight-day beast mart; the Boston Beast Market and Proclamation. Even though it is no longer held, it is still 'proclaimed' every year on 10 December in the yard of the Boston Grammar School, the Beast Yard, where the event once took place. The mayor visits and performs the short ceremony with the town clerk and the boys have the afternoon off school. The proclamation stipulates good behaviour by all throughout the duration of the mart. On a visit to the school, the staff were kind enough to give me a copy of the proclamation, which runs as follows:

> Oh Yes! Oh Yes! Oh Yes! The Right Worshipful the Mayor and Burgesses of this Borough of Boston do strictly charge and command all manner of Persons resorting to the Mart which will begin tomorrow and continue the Eight following days, to keep the peace, and that no manner of person or persons make any

The Boston Grammar School Beast Yard, where the Beast Mart was once held. The building is now the school library and the yard a playground. The library houses stained-glass windows depicting the Beast Mart Proclamation.

One of the stained-glass windows in the library of the Boston Grammar School, encompassing the Boston Stump in the background and a scene from the Beast Mart in the foreground.

quarrels or draw any weapon to that intent upon pain of imprisonment; and that no manner of person or persons walk abroad in the night during the time of the said Mart without lawful cause, but resort to their honest Booths, Houses or Lodgings upon pain of imprisonment; and that no manner of person use any unlawful games during the time of the said Mart; and that they be of good honest behaviour as becometh them, as they will answer to the contrary; also that all persons resorting to the said Mart shall, when the same is ended, depart with all their wares, as he or they offending will answer to the contrary at their perils. God Save the Queen.

I was also treated to a tour of the yard and old library building, which houses a stained-glass window depicting the ceremony, installed in 1955 when the school celebrated its quarter centenary. The building is beautiful and the staff very welcoming. It is wonderful that they keep such a tradition alive and the boys are apparently very pleased, especially as they have half a day off school.

Around mid-December there used to be an annual Lincoln Christmas Fat Stock Show for the selling of livestock, but this fair ceased in 1939. In 1982 a new mid-December Lincoln Christmas Market began, a three day event which has proved to be a very popular event indeed! Unfortunately it had to be cancelled in 2010, for the first time in twenty-eight years, due to adverse weather conditions. The snowfall was too heavy and the expected 150,000 visitors had to be told to cancel their plans.

## 21 December

Mumping St Thomas Day, although not practised anymore, was a worthwhile event that helped the poorer members of society, without seeming like charity. Women and children would visit all the houses round about to collect goods and it was known as 'mumping' or in certain areas 'Thomassin'. There was no pension given in those days and people were very proud and did not want to be seen begging, so this practice was an acceptable way of helping those less fortunate. Goods collected would include coppers, small change, potatoes, cake, spare fruit, wheat, bread, tea, old clothes, candles and blankets. The rule was that only one member per household could go and so if the mother was unable, she would send one of her children round to represent her.

This was also another day for girls to try and divine who their future partner may be, by sleeping with a peeled onion under their pillow and dreaming of their husband.

> Good Saint Thomas see me right
> Let me see my love tonight.
> In his clothes and his array
> That he wears most every day.

A popular day, 21 December is also the day of the Candle Auction at Bolingbroke. Poor Folk's Close is a piece of land, the rent from which is given to charity. Rent of the land is auctioned off every year through the custom of the auctioneer sticking a pin into a candle. The candle is lit and the bidding begins. When the flame reaches the pin, it drops out and the person who made the final bid rents the land for the next twelve months. Conditions set from the benefactors, John and Eleanor Ramsden, were that no poultry was to be kept on the land and that local Girl Guides should be allowed to camp there at Whitsun. It is an old custom that is happily kept alive.

As in all counties, there are many similarities between certain festivities, Christmas of course being one of these. Mince pies were always popular, sometimes called coffin pies because they are covered with a lid. It was thought to be lucky to eat at least twelve mince pies before Christmas Day, as then you would have a happy following twelve months, but to eat fewer meant you would only have as many months' luck as the number of pies you ate. Sounds like a good excuse to me! They also participated in a tradition of Church Sticking in December, which was an old way of decorating the church. Each family had a certain pew that they used every visit and there was a hole or loop cut into the wood at the end, where they usually hung their umbrellas or walking sticks. At Christmas time the families would decorate this area of their pew with seasonal evergreens, holly and ivy and it became quite a competitive custom which made the churches look lovely.

## 24 December

Grimsby Christmas Eve Market takes place every year. There was an old superstition in Lincolnshire that on Christmas Eve, all the animals in the stables would go down on their knees at midnight to worship the baby Jesus and show reverence for him. There seem to be many accounts of people saying this, but not as many accounts of eye witnesses.

## Christmas Day

If the sun doth shine at 12 o'clock on Christmas Day, it will be a good year for apples.

Christmas Day, a day of feasting and presents the country over, and pork pies were a favourite amongst the food in Lincolnshire as was plum cake, served in strips and dipped in beer! A Yule log, or Yule clog, was traditionally burnt on the grate throughout the festive season and if it did not burn completely over Christmas, the remains were saved and used to start the fire on the following Yule period. This was thought to guarantee continuity of good fortune for the household.

There was an annual Christmas Day swim at Cleethorpes and Grimsby Docks before dinner and in some places this still occurs, although the date can differ. It was a popular event to swim in the sea on Boxing Day, and many people still indulge in this tradition.

## New Year's Eve

New Year's Eve was apparently the day Judas was born and thus it was seen as very bad luck to start any new business on this day. Silver, wood and coal were placed outside houses ready for the first guest after midnight to bring in the New Year, and it was traditional to leave the front door open for the New Year to come in and open the back door to let the old one out. Festivities and drinking were customary, just as they are today.

Of course, Lincolnshire folk celebrate many more festivals other than those listed here, both past and present, and Maureen Sutton's *A Lincolnshire Calendar* is an excellent place for more detailed information. There are some that have been passed over here, as they are celebrated all over the country and are not particularly specific to Lincolnshire, but are still, or were, celebrated in the county none-the-less: 6 January, Twelfth Night; 20 January, St Agnes Eve; 17 March, St Patrick's Day; Spring/Summer/Autumn/Winter Equinox/Solstice; 25 March Lady Day; Lent; Palm Sunday; Maundy Thursday; Good Friday; Easter Day and Easter Monday; 19 April, Primrose Day; 23 April, St George's Day; 24 May, Empire Day; 29 May, Royal Oak Day; Ascension Day and Well Dressing; Whitsunday; Corpus Christi Eve; Father's Day; 24 June, Mid-Summer's Day; 15 July, St Swithun's Day; 1 August, Lammas Day; Chestnut Sunday in September; 20 October, Trafalgar Day; 11 November, Remembrance Sunday; 30 November, St Andrew's Day; Advent; 26 December, St Stephen's Day.

Life in the past was hard and it is pleasing to know that during each month the common folk had some pleasurable occasion to look forward to. Today we still need our breaks from a hectic work schedule or busy home life. We often choose much more sophisticated pastimes, but it is strangely comforting to know that some of the old traditions and festivals are still celebrated today with vigour and enthusiasm equal to that of our forbears.

# BIBLIOGRAPHY

## Books

Alexander, M., *British Folklore Myths and Legends* (Weidenfeld & Nicolson Ltd, 1982)

Ayto, J. & Crofton, I., *Brewer's Britain and Ireland: The History, Culture, Folklore and Etymology of 7500 Places in these Islands* (Weidenfeld & Nicolson, 2005)

Bennett, S., *A History of Lincolnshire* (Phillimore & Co. Ltd, 1999)

Briggs, K.M., *British Folk Tales and Legends, A Sampler* (Granada Publishing Ltd, 1977)

Brontë, C., *Jane Eyre* (Penguin Books, 1847)

Bygott, J., *Lincolnshire* (Robert Hale Ltd, 1950)

Cameron, K., *A Dictionary of Lincolnshire Place-Names* (English Place-Name Society, 1998)

Campion, E.G., *Lincolnshire Dialects* (Richard Kay, 1976)

Codd, D., *Mysterious Lincolnshire* (Breedon Books, 2007)

Colwell, E., *Round About and Long Ago: Tales from the English Counties* (Longman Young Books, 1972)

Crossley-Holland, K., *The Old Storie: Folk Tales from East Anglia and the Fen Country* (Colt Books Ltd, 1997)

Cryer, L.R., *Byard's Leap* (South and North Kesteven, 1996)

Cuppleditch, D., *The Lincolnshire Coast* (Sutton Publishing, 1996)

Fisk, R., *Lincoln Scrap-Book Peeps Into The Past* (Roy Fisk, 1989)

Fisk, R., *Lincolnshire Gleanings* (Roy Fisk, 1987)

Fisk, R., *Lincolnshire Medley* (Roy Fisk, 1989)

Fisk, R., *Reflecting Lincolnshire* (Roy Fisk, 1981)

Goddard, J. & Spalding, R., *Fish 'n' Ships: The Rise and Fall of Grimsby – The World's Premier Fishing Port* (Dalesman Publishing, 1987)

Gray, A., *Lincolnshire Headlines* (Countryside Books, 1993)

Gray, A., *Tales of Old Lincolnshire* (Countryside Books, 1990)

Gutch, Mrs & Peacock, M., *Examples of Printed Folk-Lore Concerning Lincolnshire* (David Nutt, 1908)

Halpenny, B.B., *Ghost Stations V, VI and Lincolnshire* (Casdec Ltd, 1993)

Hobson, J., *Curious Country Customs* (David & Charles, 2007)

*Holy Bible*, The New Revised Standard Version (Oxford University Press, 1995)

Honeybone, M., *Wicked Practise & Sorcery: The Belvoir Witchcraft case of 1619* (Baron Books, 2008)
Howat, P., *Ghosts & Legends of Lincolnshire & The Fen Country* (Countryside Books, 1992)
James, M., *From the Dead Moon to Yallery Brown, revisiting the 'Legends of the Cars'* (Folklore, 1891)
Kazimierczuk, E., *A Lincolnshire Notebook* (Hutton Press Ltd, 1991)
Kesson H.J., *The Legend of the Lincoln Imp* (J.W. Ruddock & Sons, 1904)
Ketteringham, J.R., *A Lincolnshire Hotchpotch* (J.R. Ketteringham, 1989)
Ketteringham, J.R., *A Second Lincolnshire Hotchpotch* (J.R. Ketteringham, 1990)
Ketteringham, J.R., *A Third Lincolnshire Hotchpotch* (J.R. Ketteringham, 1999)
Lazenby, C. & J., *Deep Sea Voices: Recollections of Women in our Fishing Communities* (Tempus Publishing, 1999)
*Lincolnshire Life,* The County Magazine, 1933, 1934, 1935, 1937, 1962, 1982, 1983, 1994, 1998, 1999
*Lincolnshire Poacher* magazine, 2002, 2003
Marlowe, C., *Legends of the Fenland People* (EP Publishing, 1976)
Marrows, H., *Walking Through Lincolnshire's History* (At Heart Ltd, 2008)
McLeish, K., *Myths & Folkstories of Britain & Ireland* (Longman Group UK Ltd, 1986)
Mitchell, J. with Tilney All Saints' Local History Group, *Tilney All Saints' In Living Memory* (Tilney All Saints' Local History Group, 2008)
Naylor, S., *Lincolnshire Country Life Beside the Wash 1920's to 1939* (Guardian Press, 2000)
Noble, J., *Around the Coast with Buffalo Bill: The Wild West in Yorkshire & Lincolnshire* (Hutton Press, 1999)
Palmer, R., *Britain's Living Folklore* (David & Charles, 1991)
Peach, H., *The Curiosities of England, Lincolnshire Curiosities* (The Dovecoat Press, 1994)
Peacock, M. & M., *The Peacock Lincolnshire Word Books 1884–1920* (Scunthorpe Museum Society, 1997)
Rex, P., *Hereward, The Last Englishman* (Tempus Publishing, 2005)
Robinson, D.N., *The Book of the Lincolnshire Seaside* (Barracuda Books, 1981)
Rudkin, E.H., *Lincolnshire Folklore* (Robert Pacey, 1936)
Rudkin, E.H., *The Black Dog* (Folk Lore Vol.49, 1938)
Spelman, J., *Lincolnshire Bedside Book: A Collection of Prose and Poetry* (The Dovecote Press, 2003)
Stennett, A., *Nobbut A Yellerbelly! A Salute to the Lincolnshire Dialect* (Countryside Books, 2006)
Sutton, M., *A Lincolnshire Calendar* (Paul Watkins, 1997)
Tennyson, A., *A critical Edition of the Major Works* (Oxford University Press, 2000)
Westwood, J. & Simpson, J., *The Penguin Book of Ghosts* (Penguin Group, 2005)
Westwood, J., *Albion, A Guide to Legendary Britain* (Granada Publishing, 1985)
Whistler, C.W., *Havelok The Dane: A Legend of Old Grimsby and Lincoln* (Thomas Nelson & Sons, 1900)
Whitlock, R., *Here Be Dragons* (George Allen & Unwin, 1983)
Yorke, A., *Just Hanging About: The Lincolnshire Tales* (Lindum Scribes, Lincoln)

## Websites

www.beehive.thisisgrimsby.co.uk
www.books.google.co.uk
www.capture.macaw.world.net
www.wikipedia.org
www.findarticles.com
www.forteanzoology.blogspot.com
www.forums.skadi.net
www.gwydir.demon.co.uk
www.homepage.ntlworld.com
www.homepages.which.net
www.islesproject.com
www.lcjb.cjsonline.gov.uk
www.lincolnshiregothic.blogspot.com
www.markhousby.tripod.com
www.naturalplane.blogspot.com
www.nigelfishersbriggblog.blogspot.com
www.nli.northampton.ac.uk
www.raf-lincolnshire.info
www.rogers-relics-uk.com
www.skegnessvideo.com
www.socyberty.com
www.wapedia.mobi
www.williamhusseyauthor.wordpress.com
www.abdn.ac.uk
www.archive.org
www.bbc.co.uk
www.bikerwolf.com
www.bostonstandard.co.uk
www.brigglife.co.uk
www.britannia.com
www.castleuk.net
www.cladonia.co.uk
www.eastbournehouse.co.uk
www.efdss.org
www.elyonline.co.uk
www.epwortholdrectory.org.uk
www.fenskating.co.uk
www.folkandroots.co.uk
www.folktalk.co.uk
www.forteantimes.com
www.gainsboroughuk.com
www.ghost-sighting.co.uk
www.gileslandscapes.co.uk
www.guardian.co.uk
www.hauntedplaces.co.uk
www.historic-uk.com
www.independent.co.uk
www.indigogroup.co.uk
www.information-britain.co.uk
www.jrank.org
www.lincolnshire.gov.uk
www.lincolnshirelife.co.uk
www.lincolnshirewolds.info
www.lincs-chamber.co.uk
www.literarynorfolk.co.uk
www.localriding.com
www.mayflowermaid.com
www.megalithic.co.uk
www.meltontimes.co.uk
www.mysteriousbritain.co.uk
www.mysterymag.com
www.mystical-www.co.uk
www.nickpope.net
www.northern-ghost-investigations.com
www.orpheusweb.co.uk
www.paranormaldatabase.com
www.raf-lincolnshire.info
www.rcep.org.uk
www.roadghosts.com
www.rodcollins.com
www.rootsweb.ancestry.com
www.show.me.uk
www.sleafordstandard.co.uk
www.smuggling.co.uk
www.spaldingtoday.co.uk
www.stone-circles.org.uk
www.stone-circles.org.uk
www.strangebritain.co.uk
www.tc-lethbridge.com
www.themodernantiquarian.com
www.thisisgrimsby.co.uk
www.thisisholbeach.co.uk
www.thisislincolnshire.co.uk
www.timetravel-britain.com
www.traditionalwitchcraft.net
www.trappedbymonsters.com
www.unexplainedmysteries.com
www.unexplainedstuff.com
www.urbanlincs.co.uk
www.zurichmansion.org
www.eloquentlunacy.com

# NOTES

### INTRODUCTION

1 'The Lincolnshire Poacher', traditional folk song, as cited in Judith Spelman's collection of prose and poetry, *Lincolnshire Bedside Book*, p.112.
2 Taken from John Betjeman's speech to the inaugural meeting of the Lincolnshire Association (1963) – quoted in John Ayto and Ian Crofton's *Brewer's Britain and Ireland*, p.668.
3 Quote from John Ayto and Ian Crofton's *Brewer's Britain and Ireland*, p.668.
4 *Lincolnshire Life*, June 1998, p.44.
5 Katharine M. Briggs, *British Folk Tales and Legends, A Sampler*, p.17.
6 Max & Mabel Peacock, *The Peacock Lincolnshire Word Books* 1884–1920, p.57.
7 *Lincolnshire Life*, dialect story, August 1998, p.41.
8 Alfred Lord Tennyson, *A Critical Edition of the Major Works*, p.376, 377.
9 *The Lincolnshire Poacher*, autumn 2002, p.49.
10 Marc Alexander, *British Folklore Myths and Legends*, p.179.
11 *Lincolnshire Magazine*, July/August 1935, p.165.
12 *Lincolnshire Magazine*, May/June 1937, p.151.
13 Mrs Gutch and Mabel Peacock, *Examples of Printed Folk-Lore Concerning Lincolnshire*, p.424.
14 John Ayto and Ian Crofton's *Brewer's Britain and Ireland*, p.668.
15 Jack Yates and Henry Thorold, *Lincolnshire, A Shell Guide*, as cited in Judith Spelman's collection of prose and poetry, *Lincolnshire Bedside Book*, p.12.
16 Taken from Daniel Defoe's *A tour through England and Wales, Vol.2*, 1724, when he was apparently travelling that way in beginning of eighteenth century. Cited by Judith Spelman in her collection of prose and poetry, *Lincolnshire Bedside Book*, p.66.

### 1: THE DEVIL AND HIS SERPENT

1 *Lincolnshire Life* magazine, October 1999, p.70.
2 Ethel H. Rudkin, *Lincolnshire Folklore*.
3 Ethel H. Rudkin, *Lincolnshire Folklore*, p.71.
4 Mrs Gutch and Mabel Peacock, *Examples of Printed Folk-Lore Concerning Lincolnshire*, p.65.
5 Mrs Gutch and Mabel Peacock, *Examples of Printed Folk-Lore Concerning Lincolnshire*, p.vi.
6 Quote from Thomas Fuller, *The History of the Worthies of England Vol.ii*, as cited on www.books.google.com
7 H.J. Kesson, *The Legend of the Lincoln Imp*.
8 *Lincolnshire Life*, November 1998, p.53.

9  Adrian Gray, *Tales of Old Lincolnshire*, p.22.
10 *Lincolnshire Life*, May 1998, p.19.
11 Mrs Gutch and Mabel Peacock, *Examples of Printed Folk-Lore Concerning Lincolnshire*, p.64.
12 Polly Howat, *Ghosts & Legends of Lincolnshire & The Fen Country*, p.77.
13 Daniel Codd, *Mysterious Lincolnshire*, p.43.
14 Polly Howat, *Ghosts & Legends of Lincolnshire & The Fen Country*, p.88.
15 Daniel Codd, *Mysterious Lincolnshire*, p.42.
16 Revelations 12: 7–9, The Bible.
17 Ethel H. Rudkin, *Lincolnshire Folklore*, p.56.
18 Ethel H. Rudkin, *Lincolnshire Folklore*, p.67.
19 Quote taken from Gough's *Camden*, Vol.1, p.274. Cited in *The Lincolnshire Magazine* July/August 1935, p.164.
20 Christopher Marlowe, *Legends of the Fenland People*, p.57.
21 Polly Howat, *Ghosts & Legends of Lincolnshire & The Fen Country*, p.17.
22 Adrian Gray, *Tales of Old Lincolnshire*, p.95.
23 Ralph Whitlock, *Here Be Dragons*, p.44.
24 Mrs Gutch and Mabel Peacock, *Examples of Printed Folk-Lore Concerning Lincolnshire*, p.34.
25 Isaiah 27:1, The Bible.
26 Daniel Codd, *Mysterious Lincolnshire*, p.43.

## 2: The Wet And Wilds

1  See Rex Needle's website: www.homepages.which.net
2  ibid.
3  Judith Spelman, *Lincolnshire Bedside Book: A Collection of Prose and Poetry*, p.13 quoted from Jack Yates and Henry Thorold, *Lincolnshire, A Shell Guide*.
4  Christopher Marlowe, *Legends of the Fenland People*, p.11.
5  Kenneth McLeish, *Myths & Folkstories of Britain & Ireland*, p.18.
6  Jennifer Westwood, *Albion, A Guide to Legendary Britain*, p.183.
7  Stewart Bennett, *A History of Lincolnshire*, p.85.
8  Polly Howat, *Ghosts & Legends of Lincolnshire & The Fen Country*, p.7.
9  Adrian Gray, *Tales of Old Lincolnshire*, p.114.
10 Jennifer Westwood and Jacqueline Simpson, *The Penguin Book of Ghosts*, p.217.
11 Polly Howat, *Ghosts & Legends of Lincolnshire & The Fen Country*, p.68.
12 Adrian Gray, *Tales of Old Lincolnshire*, p.54.
13 Daniel Codd, *Mysterious Lincolnshire*, p.72.
14 Elaine Kazimierczuk, *A Lincolnshire Notebook*, p.5.
15 *Lincolnshire Life*, January 1998.
16 *Lincolnshire Life*, June 1998, p.44.
17 Christopher Marlowe, *Legends of the Fenland People*, p.199.
18 John Goddard & Roger Spalding, *Fish 'n' Ships: The Rise and Fall of Grimsby – The World's Premier Fishing Port*, p.43.
19 *Lincolnshire Life*, October 1999, p.70.
20 Mrs Gutch and Mabel Peacock, *Examples of Printed Folk-Lore Concerning Lincolnshire*, p.7.
21 D.C. Staveley in David N. Robinson's, *The Book of the Lincolnshire Seaside*, p.139.
22 Polly Howat, *Ghosts & Legends of Lincolnshire & The Fen Country*, p.14.
23 Katharine M. Briggs, *British Folk Tales and Legends, A Sampler*, p.215.

## 3: Black Dogs and Strange Encounters

1. Taken from Charlotte Brontë's *Jane Eyre*, p.113/114.
2. From Theo Brown, *The Black Dog, Folk-Lore*, 1958. See www.nli.northampton.ac.uk
3. See www.paranormaldatabase.com
4. Katharine M. Briggs, *British Folk Tales and Legends, A Sampler*, p.115.
5. Ethel H. Rudkin, *The Black Dog*, p.113.
6. Poem reproduced in Ethel Rudkin, *The Black Dog*, p.119/120, written by Muriel M. Andrew, entitled 'The Legend of the Ghost in Bonny Wells Lane'.
7. Daniel Codd, *Mysterious Lincolnshire*, p.93.
8. See www.nli.northampton.ac.uk
9. See www.lincolnshiregothic.blogspot.com
10. Daniel Codd, *Mysterious Lincolnshire*, p.149.
11. ibid, p.151.
12. Christopher Marlowe, *Legends of the Fenland People*.
13. Daniel Codd, *Mysterious Lincolnshire*, p.149.
14. Mrs Gutch and Mabel Peacock, *Examples of Printed Folk-Lore Concerning Lincolnshire*, p.65 & 240.
15. Jennifer Westwood and Jacqueline Simpson, *The Penguin Book of Ghosts*, p.218.
16. *Lincolnshire Life*, December 1998, p.28.
17. Jennifer Westwood, *Albion, A Guide to Legendary Britain*, p.209.
18. Polly Howat, *Ghosts & Legends of Lincolnshire & The Fen Country*, p.36/37.

## 4: Giants and Heroes

1. Daniel Codd, *Mysterious Lincolnshire*, p.11.
2. Charles W. Whistler, *Havelok The Dane: A Legend of Old Grimsby and Lincoln*, p.117.
3. Jennifer Westwood, *Albion, A Guide to Legendary Britain*, p.191.
4. Polly Howat, *Ghosts & Legends of Lincolnshire & The Fen Country*, p.60.
5. *Lincolnshire Life*, April 1998, p.26.
6. See www.hiddenea.com
7. Daniel Codd, *Mysterious Lincolnshire*, p.155.
8. ibid, p.16.
9. Ethel H. Rudkin, *Lincolnshire Folklore*, p.64.
10. Mrs Gutch and Mabel Peacock, *Examples of Printed Folk-Lore Concerning Lincolnshire*, p.323.
11. Adrian Gray, *Tales of Old Lincolnshire*, p.118.
12. Peter Rex, *Hereward, The Last Englishman*, p.33.
13. ibid, p.26.
14. See www.robinhoodloxley.net
15. Peter Rex, *Hereward, The Last Englishman*, p.58.
16. Christopher Marlowe, *Legends of the Fenland People*, p.40.
17. Peter Rex, *Hereward, The Last Englishman*, p.67.

## 5: Things that go Bump in the Lincolnshire Night

1. See www.unexplained-mysteries.com
2. Ethel H. Rudkin, *Lincolnshire Folklore*, p.34. *Tittuppin'* means going up and down or backwards and forwards.
3. Daniel Codd, *Mysterious Lincolnshire*, p.88/94.
4. *The Lincolnshire Magazine*, July/August 1935, p.165.

5 Daniel Codd, *Mysterious Lincolnshire*, p.94. *See also* www.orpheusweb.co.uk
6 Ethel H. Rudkin, *Lincolnshire Folklore*, p.29.
7 *Lincolnshire Life*, January 1994, p.10.
8 Roy Fisk, *Lincolnshire Medley*, p.102.
9 From *The Gentleman's Magazine*, Vol.130 (1821). Extract of description given by Mr Gervase Hollis (from Grimsby) about 1640 (Harleian MSS No.6829 p.162).
10 *See* www.rodcollins.com
11 Ethel H. Rudkin, *Lincolnshire Folklore*, p.30.
12 Christopher Marlowe, *Legends of the Fenland People*, p.189.
13 Mrs Gutch and Mabel Peacock, *Examples of Printed Folk-Lore Concerning Lincolnshire*, p.50.
14 Polly Howat, *Ghosts & Legends of Lincolnshire & The Fen Country*, p.79.
15 *See* Daniel Codd's website: www.urbanlincs.co.uk
16 *Lincolnshire Life*, September 1998, p.70.
17 Mrs Gutch and Mabel Peacock, *Examples of Printed Folk-Lore Concerning Lincolnshire*, p.50.
18 *The Lincolnshire Magazine*, May/June 1934, p.362.
19 *Lincolnshire Life* magazine, October 1998, p.70.

## 6: Witchcraft and Cunning

1 *See* www.bibliotecapleyades.net
2 Ethel H. Rudkin, *Lincolnshire Folklore*.
3 Mrs Gutch and Mabel Peacock, *Examples of Printed Folk-Lore Concerning Lincolnshire*, p.96.
4 Daniel Codd, *Mysterious Lincolnshire*, p.50.
5 Mrs Gutch and Mabel Peacock, *Examples of Printed Folk-Lore Concerning Lincolnshire*, p.91/197. 'Eyespell' is presumably some sort of curse, although not fully explained.
6 Mrs Gutch and Mabel Peacock, *Examples of Printed Folk-Lore Concerning Lincolnshire*, p.97.
7 Katharine M. Briggs, *British Folk Tales and Legends, A Sampler*, p.304.
8 Daniel Codd, *Mysterious Lincolnshire*, p.48.
9 Mrs Gutch and Mabel Peacock, *Examples of Printed Folk-Lore Concerning Lincolnshire*, p.78.
10 *Lincolnshire Life*, October 1998, p.70.
11 Mrs Gutch and Mabel Peacock, *Examples of Printed Folk-Lore Concerning Lincolnshire*, p.54.
12 Katharine M. Briggs, *British Folk Tales and Legends, A Sampler*, p.194.
13 Daniel Codd, *Mysterious Lincolnshire*, p.47.
14 Gutch and Mabel Peacock, *Examples of Printed Folk-Lore Concerning Lincolnshire*, p.81.
15 Jennifer Westwood, *Albion, A Guide to Legendary Britain*, p.181.
16 Mrs Gutch and Mabel Peacock, *Examples of Printed Folk-Lore Concerning Lincolnshire*, p.97/98.

## 7: Yellowbelly Sayings and Superstitions

1 Roy Fisk, *Lincolnshire Gleanings*, p.69.
2 *Lincolnshire Life*, May 1998, p.19.
3 *Lincolnshire Life*, April 1998, p.26.
4 Roy Palmer, *Britain's Living Folklore*, p.67.
5 G. Edward Campion, *Lincolnshire Dialects*, p.31.

6 Roy Palmer, *Britain's Living Folklore*, p.77.
7 *Lincolnshire Life*, January 1999, p.12.
8 *Lincolnshire Life*, June 1999, p.23.
9 Katharine M. Briggs, *British Folk Tales and Legends, A Sampler*, p.266.
10 Mrs Gutch and Mabel Peacock, *Examples of Printed Folk-Lore Concerning Lincolnshire*, p.29.
11 Ethel H. Rudkin, *Lincolnshire Folklore*, p.20.
12 Mrs Gutch and Mabel Peacock, *Examples of Printed Folk-Lore Concerning Lincolnshire*, p.150.
13 Ethel H. Rudkin, *Lincolnshire Folklore*, p.15.
14 Mrs Gutch and Mabel Peacock, *Examples of Printed Folk-Lore Concerning Lincolnshire*, p.22.
15 *The Lincolnshire Magazine*, July/August 1935, p.164.
16 Daniel Codd, *Mysterious Lincolnshire*, p.180.
17 ibid, p.181.
18 Mrs Gutch and Mabel Peacock, *Examples of Printed Folk-Lore Concerning Lincolnshire*, p.2/3.
19 ibid, p.40/43.
20 ibid, p.38.
21 ibid, p.22.
22 ibid, p.37.
23 ibid, p.156.
24 *The Lincolnshire Poacher* magazine quoted from Mrs E. M. Shafto, autumn 2002, p.58.
25 Mrs Gutch and Mabel Peacock, *Examples of Printed Folk-Lore Concerning Lincolnshire*, p.13.
26 Roy Fisk *Lincolnshire Gleanings*, p.42 & 69.
27 *The Lincolnshire Poacher*, quoted from Andrew Allen's article, autumn 2002, p.30.

## 8: A Lincolnshire Year

1 Maureen Sutton, *A Lincolnshire Calendar*.
2 Mrs Gutch and Mabel Peacock, *Examples of Printed Folk-Lore Concerning Lincolnshire*, p.169.
3 Ethel H. Rudkin, *Lincolnshire Folklore*, p.41.
4 ibid, p.49.
5 ibid, p.92.
6 Elaine Kazimierczuk, *A Lincolnshire Notebook*, p.8.
7 Hobson, Jeremy: *Curious Country Customs*, p.14.
8 Mrs Gutch and Mabel Peacock, *Examples of Printed Folk-Lore Concerning Lincolnshire*, p.188.
9 *Lincolnshire Life* magazine, April 1999, p.7.
10 Ethel H. Rudkin, *Lincolnshire Folklore*, p.45.
11 Mrs Gutch and Mabel Peacock, *Examples of Printed Folk-Lore Concerning Lincolnshire*, p.193.
12 *See* J.D.A. Widdowson's website: www.eastbournehouse.co.uk
13 Ethel H. Rudkin, *Lincolnshire Folklore*, p.46.
14 *The Lincolnshire Magazine*, September/October 1934, p.14.
15 *Lincolnshire Life*, October 1998, p.70.
16 Mrs Gutch and Mabel Peacock, *Examples of Printed Folk-Lore Concerning Lincolnshire*, p.212.

# INDEX

Alkborough 151

Anwick 34, 36

Bardney 142, 143, 169
Barton 109, 169
bees 137
Belvoir 116, 117, 118, 119, 183
Bigby 81
birth 99, 133, 136, 139, 144, 157
black dog 10, 63–75, 102, 128, 183, 187
Blyborough 64
bogles 10, 49, 50, 51
Bolingbroke Castle 14, 100, 101
Boston 7, 14, 25, 51, 99, 101, 108, 145, 158, 167, 177, 178
Boston Stump 25, 51, 99, 101, 145, 167, 178
Bottesford 58, 71, 118, 119, 120
Bourne 70, 85, 86, 162, 167
Bourne Wood 65
Bradley Woods 98, 99, 172
Bransby 66, 67, 102
Brigg 47, 48, 59, 66, 166, 170
Burgh-le-Marsh 59, 60
Buslingthorpe 38
Byard's Leap 129, 130

Cadeby Hall 109
Caistor 58, 92, 106, 152, 160
Carr 45, 49, 50
Castle Carlton 36, 37
Cleethorpes 132, 180
Coningsby 132, 157
Cornelius Vermuyden 45
Cranwell 129, 130
Crosby 20

Crowland 30, 31, 41, 71
Crowland Abbey 30
cunning 115–130

dead cart 139
Dead Hand 48, 49
Death 10, 12, 45, 57, 60, 64, 115, 116, 119, 133, 136–140, 152, 153, 159, 164
decoy ducks 18
Devil 8, 10, 20–40, 41, 48, 55, 65, 83, 102, 117, 124, 133, 135, 136, 173
Devil's Pulpit 21, 22, 23
Devil's Stone 35
dialect 11, 13, 14, 151
Digby 15, 109,
Dogdyke 7, 70, 71
Dorrington 20, 22, 29, 126
dragon 10, 31–40, 173
Dragonby 34, 39, 40
Drake Stone 32, 33, 34, 35

East Halton 93
elder 123, 139, 140
Ely 87, 88, 89, 140
Epworth Rectory 90, 92, 166
Etheldreda 140, 141, 167

fairies 47, 119, 123, 133
familiar 30, 54, 117, 118
Fan 'o the Fens 54, 55, 56
Fen 17, 41, 42, 44, 45–7, 51, 52, 54–6, 62, 70, 71, 85–9, 106, 110, 123, 124, 126, 131, 132
Fen Slodgers 52, 132
Fillingham Castle 97

# INDEX

First Footing 152
Fishtoft 143, 144, 145
flood laws 62
Fonaby Top 75
Frieston 27
Fulletby 93

Gainsborough 68, 95, 96, 135, 157, 158, 169
Gainsborough Old Hall 95, 96
Gedney 69, 134
ghosts 10, 47, 65, 66, 90–114, 124, 128
giants 10, 76–89
Girsby 110, 127
Grantham 14, 116, 117, 160
Grasby 128
Green Mist 49
greencoaties 46
Grim 76, 77, 78
Grimsby 7, 14, 56, 76–9, 109, 172, 180
Gunby Hall 95, 96
Gunthorpe 102

Halloween 25, 102, 115, 124, 173
Harmston Hall 97, 98
Havelok 77, 78
Haxey 7, 76, 153, 154, 155, 156
Haxey Hood 7, 153–6
Hemswell 22, 23, 68, 165
Hengist 44, 45
Hereward 14, 85–9
Holbeach 102–4, 169–70
Horncastle 21, 35, 93, 138, 167, 170
Horsington 8, 173, 174

Iceni 42–4
imp 22, 24–6, 28, 83, 102, 117
Ingoldmells 140
Irby Dale Woods 97, 98
Isle of Axholme 82, 90

Jesus 75, 157, 159, 161, 162, 180
John Barleycorn 156

King Arthur 15
King John 58, 59
King Vortigern 44

King's Lynn 32, 33, 80
Kirton-in-Lindsey 58, 72, 126

Lacky Causey Calf 48
Lincoln 7, 13, 14–18, 22, 24, 25–7, 38, 55, 58, 77, 94, 95, 104, 105, 117, 118, 121, 122, 124, 132, 133, 142, 153, 156, 157, 158, 159, 162, 163, 164, 165, 166, 167, 168, 171, 172, 176, 179
Lincoln Cathedral 7, 13, 16, 22, 24, 26, 104, 105, 142, 159, 166, 167, 176
Lincoln Green 132
Lincolnshire Poacher 10
Lindholme 28, 82, 83
Long Tom Pattison 48
Louth 36, 37, 54, 56, 61, 108, 124, 127, 158, 162, 163
luck 10, 27, 29, 36, 57, 58, 75, 93, 123, 131, 133, 136, 139, 145, 146, 147, 149, 150, 152, 162, 163, 164, 179, 180
Ludford 128

Mablethorpe 58, 59, 60, 168
Malleus Maleficarum 116
Mandru 43, 44
Manton 66
Manwar Rings 29, 30
marriage 14, 45, 73, 91, 133–6, 138, 147
Messingham 121
Min-mim 47
Molly Grime 160
Monks Abbey 53, 55
moon 20, 46, 50, 51, 55, 69, 70, 100, 136, 145, 147, 149
Moortown Hall 66
morris dancers 153, 165
Mr Fox 73, 74
Mr Lacy 74
Mumby 146

Navenby 121, 122, 137
Normanby-by-Spital 93
Northorpe 70, 128
Old Lad 20, 21

Old Mother Nightshade 69
Old Nick 20, 25, 27, 35
Ormsby 37, 38

plough jags 153
poltergeist 68, 90, 92, 93

Quadring 27

RAF Scampton 7, 111, 113, 114
Raveley 27
Ravendale 104
Read's Island 68, 69
Renwein 45
Revesby 124
riding the stang 135
Roman 16, 42, 43, 44, 45, 76, 114, 128
Rowston 127

sack stones 75
St Botolph 25, 26, 124, 125, 167
St Guthlac 36, 143, 144
St Hugh 24, 26, 36, 37, 112, 176
St Mark's Eve 21, 134, 164
Satan 27, 30, 31, 32, 83, 124
Saxby 128
Saxilby 94
Scamblesby 15, 128
Scunthorpe 34, 48
serpent 20, 32, 37, 38, 40
shagfoal 64
shape shifting 126, 127
ship-wrecking 59
Sir Hugh Barde 36, 37
Skegness 15, 106, 107, 140, 167, 168
Skidbrooke 124, 125
Slash Hollow 35
Sleaford 93, 115
smuggling 59
South Ferriby 72

Southery 62
Spalding 68
Stamford 58, 89, 160, 169, 176
Stickney 174
Stow 141, 142, 167, 168
Swineshead 8, 30, 138

Tatter Foal 48
Tealby 8, 21, 23
Tennyson 13, 14, 95
Tetford 127
Thorpe Hall 99
Tiddy Mun 45, 46, 47
Tom Hickathrift 78, 79, 80, 83
Tom Otter 93, 94, 95
Tommy Lindrum 28
Tyrwhitt 81, 82

Wash, the 41, 52, 58, 59, 78, 169–70
weather (lore) 52, 58, 131, 133, 147, 148, 149, 158, 162
werewolf 68, 70, 71
Wesley 14, 58, 90, 91, 92, 166
Wild Man of the Woods 81
Wildsworth 53
William of Lindholme 82
Will-o-the-Wisps 47, 48, 50
Willoughton 21, 121
Winceby 35
witch 7, 10, 20, 22, 29, 30, 45, 50, 54–6, 64, 69–71, 89, 91, 100, 115–130, 140, 147
witches of Belvoir 116

Yaddlethorpe 71, 123
Yallery Brown 72, 73
yellowbelly 10, 131, 132

zombies 71